Verle Hoffman

You Can WITNESS
With CONFIDENCE

BOOKS BY ROSALIND RINKER . . .

The Years That Count

Who Is This Man?

Becoming a Christian

You Can Witness With Confidence

PRAYER — Conversing With God

Communicating Love Through Prayer

by ROSALIND RINKER

You Can
WITNESS With
CONFIDENCE

ZONDERVAN PUBLISHING HOUSE
Grand Rapids, Michigan

YOU CAN WITNESS WITH CONFIDENCE
Copyright 1962 by
Zondervan Publishing House
Grand Rapids, Michigan

First printing..........May, 1962
Second printing...November, 1962
Third printing........April, 1963
Fourth printing...December, 1963
Fifth printing..........May, 1964
Sixth printing.....November, 1964
Seventh printing.......April, 1965
Eighth printing........April, 1966
Ninth printing.........July, 1966
Tenth printing......October, 1966

90,000 copies in print

Printed in the United States of America

To

EUGENIA PRICE

My friend and associate,
who encouraged me to start writing.

The very spring of our actions is the love of Christ. We look at it like this: if one died for all men, then in a sense, they all died, and his purpose in dying for them is that their lives should now be no longer lived for themselves but for him who died and rose again for them. . . . For if a man is in Christ he becomes a new person altogether — the past is finished and gone, everything has become fresh and new. All this is God's doing, for he has reconciled us to himself through Jesus Christ; and he has made us agents of the reconciliation. God was in Christ personally reconciling the world to himself — not counting their sins against them — and has commissioned us with the message of reconciliation. We are now Christ's ambassadors, as though God were appealing direct to you through us. As his personal representative, we say, "Make your peace with God."

For God caused Christ, who himself knew nothing of sin, actually to *be* sin for our sakes, so that in Christ we might be made good with the goodness of God.

2 Corinthians 5:14-21
Phillips' Translation

Preface

THIS IS THE STORY OF HOW I LEARNED TO WITNESS. IT IS A continuous story. If you happen to jump into the middle of some chapter, you may feel like saying, "This author is a heretic!" I'm not a heretic at all. I love Jesus Christ and I belong to Him. He's given me courage to put aside what does not work, and through His Spirit of love, has taught me what can and does work. Even so, there is still much to learn.

To many persons, witnessing is looked upon as an obligation or a tremendous burden. Moreover, it puts them into great bondage. They feel condemned if they are not constantly forcing the issue with someone. This paralyzing fear stems from a misconception of what it means to be a witness to Jesus Christ. Too many of us are witnesses to our own religious experience. Jesus said, "Ye shall be witnesses unto Me."

When we learn the secrets of being a witness to Jesus Christ, we learn the difference between being an objective and a subjective witness. Love is the first requisite. Love teaches us (a) when to speak of Christ and who He is, and (b) when to speak of the difference His Presence makes in daily living and relationships.

In today's fast moving world we still cling to antiquated outlines and methods of personal evangelism written or prepared 50 to 100 years ago. It is time we forgot "methods" and return to the subject matter used 2000 years ago: *The living, resurrected Jesus Christ.*

I would like to express my thanks to Eugenia Price for her attention to content; to Johnny Erickson for typing the manuscript; and to Carol M. Williams, Captain, United States Air Force, for her aid in editing these chapters, for being my severest critic, and for reminding me to identify with all my readers.

Christianity is Christ. Witnessing to Him is exciting and full of surprises, as I hope you will agree when you have read this book.

ROSALIND RINKER

Chicago, Illinois.

CONTENTS

PART I

Love
Is
the
First
Requisite

CHAPTER 1

My First Witness

I remember the first time I witnessed to another person about Jesus Christ. I was fifteen years old. Myrtle was my high-school friend, with whom I walked to school every morning.

On what basis could I appeal to her? Where should I start? Because start I must: a not-to-subtle pressure was being applied by the minister's wife upon a number of us teen-agers. "If you are really saved, you will tell others and bring them to Jesus."

Tell them what? That I was saved and that they could be "saved" too? I wasn't sure my friend Myrtle was interested in "being saved." At that point, I'm sure I wouldn't have been able to tell you just why, but I knew she wasn't.

And what then would she be interested in? And where do you think I started?

I have to smile, and chuckle a bit to myself, as I write this, and I wonder where you started, when you first tried to witness for Jesus Christ. Anyway, a start is better than no start at all!

Our conversation one morning, when I took my courage in hand, ran something like this:

"Myrtle, did you ever read the 24th chapter of Matthew?"

"Well — no. I don't remember that I ever did. Why?"

"Oh — on Sunday I heard our minister preach from that chapter. It talks about the end of the world. And what is going to happen to people!"

"The end of the world? What is going to happen?"

From there it was simple. I told her about the two people in bed together — one was taken up into the air to meet Jesus, and the other was left alone in bed! I told her about the two men working in the field—one was taken "up" and one was left standing in the field! I told her about the two women shopping in a super-market (grinding at the mill) when one of them just disappeared and the other one couldn't find her!

Did she want to be one of those left behind? Alone?

Did she? She did not. Right there I told her how I gave my heart to Jesus Christ, and that she could give hers to Jesus too, and be ready to meet Him when He came in the clouds of the sky. And she did.

A few months ago, I received an unexpected letter from Minnesota, and it was from Myrtle. After losing track of her all these years! Somewhere she got a copy of my book, *Prayer, Conversing with God,* and wrote to tell me how much it meant to her. She had married, had eight children and eleven grandchildren. And she wrote, "How good God is, Rosalind, to let your life influence me all these years. First, in bringing me to Christ, and now through your book, enriching my life again."

Yes, God is good. And isn't it wonderfully encouraging and comforting to know that He uses all our attempts to do His will? We can try anything with a sincere heart, and be sure He will use as much of it as He possibly can.

────────

For thoughtful discussion:
1. Read the first sentence again. Discuss the motivation and the subject matter.
2. Do you think it is a good subject for a witness?
3. Do you think I witnessed to Jesus Christ?
4. What do you think it means to "witness to Jesus Christ"?

CHAPTER 2

Witnessing to My Religious Vocabulary

After that first trial witness (which by grace turned out all right) my memory seems a bit hazy. I really can't remember anything very definite in the way of another teen-aged person-to-person witness. I do remember, as I began to be acquainted with the typical evening evangelistic service in the church, that I began to despair of ever bringing any more of my high-school friends to Christ.

The more I saw and heard of hell-fire sermons, with hair-raising illustrations of people rejecting God, the long-drawn-out invitations urging people to go forward, and watching them stand stubbornly in their places, the more I despaired. If my friends came to church with me once, they found excuses not to come again. They even said their mothers wouldn't let them go! What was I to do? I was willing to help them, and they weren't willing to be helped. Jesus was willing to help them, and they weren't willing to be helped.

What could I do? Right from the moment of my conversion, God has given me a strong sense of responsibility for others. Because I didn't know what to do, I did the only thing left to do. I said to myself what I'd heard the minister say in his sermons, and tried to persuade myself it was true. I said, "Well, they've hardened their hearts against the Lord, and the devil has taken the gospel seed away." And with that rationalized excuse, I comforted myself.

The next thing I remember about any attempt at witnessing was door-to-door visitation. After I graduated from high school, my parents felt I should have a year or so at a Bible school before going to college, in order to "ground me in the faith," because people who went to college (I was told) usually lost their faith. So off I went to Bible School.

I took a course in Personal Evangelism, learned pages of out-

15

lines, with potential situations, and memorized reams of Bible verses to meet them. We were then sent out two-by-two to knock on doors, distribute literature and do personal evangelism for so many hours each week as part of our training.

This kind of witnessing, to unknown people who would open a door, was much easier than trying to win my personal friends to Christ. When people gave us certain excuses, we were to pull out our mental notebooks, pick out the right answer, and give them what the Bible said. We were to be sure not to give them human reasons, because human reasoning was not enough. We were to give them the Word of God. The Holy Spirit would make that stick in their minds, because God said, "My word shall not return unto me void."

For instance, if we knocked at a door and asked if we might come in and read the Bible to them, the woman at the door might answer, "Sorry, but we don't have time this morning, we're awfully busy and the children aren't dressed."

The answer would be "But lady, you have to take time to die, because the Bible says, 'It is appointed unto man once to die, and after that the judgment.'"

Or, if we knocked at a door, and a man opened it, we might introduce ourselves, and then say, "We'd like to come in and talk to you about God's qualifications for getting to heaven. Have you ever been saved?" And he might reply, "We've been confirmed and we go to church sometimes." Our answer would be, "The Bible says in John 3:3, except a man be born again, he cannot see the kingdom of God. You must be born again. Confirmation and church attendance will not save you."

You've probably seen books giving answers like these. Or perhaps you've studied them in a class? And maybe you too have used these methods? And maybe for you it worked? One thing is sure, *all* the promises are true. God does use His Word. It does not return to Him empty and void, and it will accomplish His purposes. This I firmly and reverently believe.

But this early teaching merely seemed to emphasize getting the Bible verse with its content into the air, so it could get into the ear, and, we hoped, into the heart of the hearer. Some words, we were told, needed to be said aloud, like: born-again, death, judgment, being converted.

There was little, if any, attention given to the individual, where he was in his thinking, how to find an opening in his heart, how to identify with him, or how to discern where the Holy Spirit was already at work in his life.

I hesitate to write as I have. And I hesitate to leave it here to be printed, because I know books and courses like these are still being studied, and good people are still using these methods. And I do not belittle anything or any person or any way God uses, for I have clearly stated, that in His goodness, He will use any sincere-hearted person as His witness.

At any rate, this was how I started as a teen-ager. And it was from this rigidly impersonal approach that gradually I came to see where the true emphasis should be placed.

What you are now about to read is: My search for the central truth of Christianity and how God is teaching me some of *His ways* to reach the hearts of people for whom Christ gave His life.

————————

For further study:
1. Why do you think it was easier for me to witness to strangers than to my friends?
2. What were some of the things lacking in the door-to-door approach?
3. What answers would you have given to those people?

CHAPTER 3

My Compulsion to Witness

There is another story I want to tell you, which like an unfinished symphony remains in my mind. Only the opening chords were played. There was no development of the theme. This incident really shook me, and I began to search for reality in witnessing; for a way to end the nameless fear which paralyzed me when I failed to "witness." More than anything in the world, I wanted to be a skillful, loving witness for the Lord Jesus. Surely there must be a way!

The incident took place in Korea at a beautiful summer vacation spot, long before the Korean conflict. I was in my late twenties and secretary to a missionary society in China. It was natural to make friends with others of my age and profession. I've forgotten her name, but we'll call her Emily, and she was with a Canadian Mission. Recalling earlier religious training I felt reasonably sure the term "born again" was not in common use in her church. Hence, my decision to ask her a question some morning as we walked to or from the little chapel looking out over the China Sea.

I had been taught not to ask, "Are you a Christian?" since nearly everyone believed he was a Christian because he was born in a Christian land. After further thought, I decided, "Have you ever been born again?" would be a better question than, "Are you born again?" (As though there were any real difference!)

The asking of this question became an obsession with me. Each time I saw her, or was with her, I thought only of this one question, and how I might get it into our conversation. As time went on, there seemed to be no way. I could find no "leads" at all.

The very last day of our vacation came. The very last time we would walk down the path from the chapel to where our paths branched, and we would say good-by. It was my very last time to ask *that* question. The compulsion was so strong by this time, that I could think of nothing else. If I failed now, I would fail God. It would mean that I did not believe that He could help me. I would be guilty of unbelief, disobedience and procrastination. I would be a failure as a witness for Him. I must ask that question if it killed me!

We walked in silence toward the place where the little paths separated. Now was the time. It was now or never. I wince to think that in the end it was my sense of being a failure that made me ask it. It was not out of any real concern for Emily.

"Emily, have you ever been born again?"

"No, I never have."

We walked a few more steps in silence, came to the parting place, said good-by, and walked out of each other's lives.

As I walked away from her, it was with a sense of relief. I had done it! It was over! Not until much later that evening did I stop to think that what I had done was a selfish, self-centered thing to bolster my own ego. I had "witnessed."

But what had I actually done? Witnessed to what? Well, hadn't I used the words, "born again?" And wouldn't God bring those words back to her, and wouldn't they mean something to her? Something God could use? A voice within me answered, "How can they mean something to her unless she knows the meaning back of them which you know?"

It was another whole week before I dared again face the subject, even in my own mind. And then I put it quickly away. It was very much later when I actually faced what was really wrong with my purpose, my attitude and thinking, my whole approach.

I had anticipated a "no" answer, but because of fear, I was totally unprepared for any kind of an intelligent conversation. I had fallen into the same "follow-the-leader" game when it came to witnessing, that I had fallen into regarding the matter of impersonal, long-winded prayers (the subject matter of my book, *Prayer - Conversing With God.*) I was doing what I had been told and taught. I had not dared to stop and think for myself, nor let myself be taught by the Spirit. I was too afraid of being different! And "being different" might be something as heretical as "being liberal," whatever that meant.

I had not yet quietly studied the words of Jesus and the Acts of the Apostles long enough to find out that a witness spoke of the resurrected living Lord Jesus — and that a testimony spoke convincingly of the specific changes wrought within me by His new life.

But I was ready for God to teach me that my need was to have *His* kind of love for people. Love that identified with *their* need and looked at things from their standpoint, not simply counting scalps and congratulating myself that I'd "witnessed" because certain words had been said.

I was ready to learn.

————————

For thoughtful discussion:

1. What profitable conversation could one continue after asking the question, "Are you a Christian?"
2. Discuss, point by point, what was wrong with my purpose, my attitude and thinking, my whole approach. Give the positive, creative ideas in each case.
3. Using the term "born again," what possible conversation could there have been between Emily and myself, with the "no" answer? With a "yes" answer?

CHAPTER 4

God Gave Me Eyes to See

I went to China as a missionary secretary when I was only twenty years old. Through a serious illness, a story too long to relate, and eight years in the office, I did become a "real missionary." By a real missionary, I mean one who actually goes into rural areas where white people are a curiosity, and where scarcely anyone has heard of Christianity.

There were six of us in the little evangelistic band which set out for the mountains of northern Hopei Province. We were going to spend the summer months preaching to the mountain people. This would also get us out of the heat of the plains. Two missionaries, Miss Orpha Gould (a Presbyterian nurse), myself (working then with the Oriental Missionary Society), three young Chinese women who were trained workers, and a retired business man (now in his seventies) with a face like Saint John the beloved, made up our party.

The prolonged years I'd spent in the missionary office left my Chinese very sketchy, but I was learning. I could not yet cope with ideas in this language so knew there was no hope of being able to speak or teach in meetings. However, I found comfort in the thought I could at least be friendly and learn the ways of the Chinese people. All too soon I was to find I didn't even know how to do this!

At that time I had a number of misconceptions of what it meant to be a witness. One, that unless I could speak Chinese fluently I couldn't be a witness. I was not yet aware of the tremendous power an unconscious witness could be in the lives of others. I thought words, spoken words, were the means of witnessing. And I couldn't speak! Another was, that being a witness meant telling people *how* to be saved and about the *plan* of salvation. But word barriers made even this impossible to me.

However, God was about to show me in a never-to-be-forgot-

ten lesson that one of the first qualifications for being His witness
was "eyes to see the heart-needs of another person."

Orpha had gone out on some business and I was alone in the
little Chinese room we shared. The only place to sit was on the
long brick bed. I decided to "do my nails" and got out my
nail-file.

I heard footsteps and a wavering voice called, *"Yo run tsai
chia ma?"* (Is anyone at home?) There was an old grandmother,
on her little bound feet, in her dark blue pants and jacket, peer-
ing at me from watery eyes, used to long hours of weeping.

"Where is the nurse?"

I explained she was out, but would soon be back.

The old lady said she would wait and perched herself on the
wooden ledge of the brick bed. I continued "doing my nails"
with a side glance at her every once in a while. She just sat
there patiently.

After about 20 minutes, Orpha returned. Her eyes and her
face lit up with a welcoming smile, as she extended both hands
for the brown claw-like hands of the little old lady. Together
they perched on the wooden ledge of the brick bed. Despite my
limited knowledge of Chinese, I managed to follow the gist of
their conversation by listening intently.

How was she? Had she been well? How was her family?
How was her daughter? And with that last question, the little
old lady burst into tears and sobbing, wiping ineffectually at her
eyes with a kind of cloth fastened under her arm at the place
her jacket buttoned.

There they sat, and Orpha comforted her, prayed for her, and
listened to her story. More than a year before, her 20-year-old
daughter had gone to the big city to attend school. Each month
the old mother sent her a sum of money. And only recently had
the mother learned there was no "school." Instead, the daughter
was living with a man who used the old woman's money to live
on! From the depths of a saddened heart she quietly sobbed out
the entire sordid story. Yet after awhile she left, comforted and
whole in spirit.

After Orpha filled in details I'd missed, I was silent. For half
an hour I'd been with her, and I'd been "doing my nails." Only
when Orpha came in with an open heart, did this troubled heart
open in return.

"More interested in taking care of yourself?" The still small

Voice within me was speaking. "Or will you give yourself to Me, so My love in you can go out unhindered at any time, any place, to my little ones? You couldn't have preached to her because you don't know the language, but you could have listened to her story."

That afternoon, alone on the high wall surrounding the little city, I promised God I would always have time. That whenever I found myself alone with one other person, I would let His Spirit alert me to being a channel for His love. I would put my own thoughts and affairs aside, and give myself and my attention to that person. I resolved to be as wide open toward people and their need as I am toward God Himself.

Jesus' love for people took on new meaning for me that day. He always had time. He always saw through to any heart-need. And He always was ready, with a word, a touch of love and of healing.

That day I learned the importance of having heart-eyes to see the needs of others, and through Christ's love to reach my hands toward them with compassion and understanding.

_____

For meditation and prayer:

Have you made these commitments:
1. Eyes to see the heart-needs of others?
2. Leisure from yourself to sense another's need?
3. Willingness to let God's love come through you at any time, any place, with a person of any race?

CHAPTER 5

Learning to Wait

After the mountain trip, I settled down in the city of Peiping, to study the Chinese language. First of all, I wanted a little apartment of my own, so it could be furnished Chinese-style. I wanted the people who came to feel at home, so it would be easier for them to speak from their hearts. I found a suitable room, being used for storage, on our compound. A paper-hanger was called in to transform the place with his tall stacks of little white sheets.

I was busy clearing up junk in one corner, while he started papering in the other. Suddenly I remembered my decision in the mountains — to be aware of another person near me and to reach out to them with Christ's love. And right there, in the debris on the floor I saw a little red booklet. It was the gospel of John.

"Give it to the paper-hanger," a voice said within me.

I glanced over at him. Then, crossing the room I extended the booklet to him with both hands, an oriental gesture designating a gift. He looked at me, at the book, wiped his hands on his apron, and with a slight bow, accepted it with both hands.

"Sir, if you'll read the contents of this Book, you will never die."

"Never die?" he repeated after me. "Thank you. Thank you very much." And he tucked it safely away in an inner pocket and went on putting up the little square sheets.

Well, I told myself, I didn't exactly learn any of his needs, but I felt God's love in my heart for him. Silently as I continued to clear out the junk, I prayed for him, asking God to remind him of the little book when he got home that night.

Two days later, one of our Chinese pastors stopped me as I walked past the chapel. "Miss Rinker, do you remember the paper hanger who did your rooms? We just had a long talk, and he and his whole family have become believers in Jesus."

He went on to explain that upon reaching home, the man read and pondered the little book. Then gathering his family about him, he read it aloud — not once — but twice.

Deep gratefulness filled my heart, and amazement too. I really had said nothing. I had prayed for him and had courteously handed him the gospel of John. What goes on in the heart counts far more than one realizes. It was the knowledge of Jesus written by John which reached this family, not my testimony. God was revealing much to me and I was determined to keep an open and receptive heart.

At last the two-room apartment was ready and I moved in. One morning while I was studying Chinese and getting ready for my afternoon language teacher, God had another important lesson for me.

A carpenter was working in my room on a cupboard. I had been studying a half-hour or so, when a recurring thought kept pushing into my consciousness. "Well, aren't you going to talk to the carpenter? Remember the paper-hanger. You better do something."

Yes, I'd better do something. I considered a moment. Do what? Not a lot of religious talking, even though I now knew some religious words in Chinese. Not that.

What was the carpenter's need? I found myself praying to the One who knew the heart of this man. And as I prayed, the "nudging" I'd felt in my thoughts became strongly insistent.

"Well, how long are you going to wait? He's there."

With a flash of insight, I remembered Jesus' words, "My sheep know My voice and they follow Me." I recognized that the voice speaking was *not* the Shepherd's Voice! With relief, I inwardly turned to Jesus and said, "Lord, I don't believe it was You who spoke. You never push, and You're never in a hurry. You know I'm ready to do everything You want me to do. Please give me the patience of a quiet heart that I may hear *You* when *You* are ready to speak."

With that, I settled down at my desk and for two solid hours forgot all about the carpenter. Later, I entered the other room for something, and there he was, still working on the cupboard. Before returning to my desk I stopped to inspect and to comment on his work. Then it happened.

"Lady, would you mind telling me about that poster above the table. I can read. And I've been going over and over those words, but I don't understand the meaning."

For more Chinese atmosphere above the square Chinese table, I had hung a poster-picture with two scrolls on either side. The empty cross was there, nails, a hammer, a crown of thorns, a whip, and verses referring to Christ's death and to His resurrection.

Two hours of waiting! Two hours of God's timing! As best I could, I told him about Jesus. Who He was and why He came to earth. He listened intently without interruption. Then we knelt together and I taught Him to pray. He was ready. God had opened his heart.

I was learning. Learning God's ways. Learning that God's opening of our hearts does not require our deliberate effort but rather quietly awaiting the time He appoints. Nothing out of God's timing works. I was learning the importance of keeping in touch with God through my heart. That He would bring people to me through everyday contacts with their hearts already open. I was learning that if I waited, clues as to where to begin would come right from the person concerned. I was suddenly appalled by all the clutter I had spread in people's minds! How much better it was to wait. To learn what they were thinking. And then to move into a conversation meaningful for them.

Those incidents took all my old fears out of witnessing. By waiting, I began to trust and to anticipate with eagerness what God would do. I found I didn't need to condemn myself for not witnessing on certain occasions. Instead, all I had to do was say, "Lord, I'm ready." I also found a new prayer often on my lips: "Lord, lead me to the person in whom your Spirit is already at work."

————————

For study or meditation:
1. "The heart that is to be filled to the brim with holy joy must be held still." Bowes.
2. Make a list of new lessons learned in this chapter.
3. Read Acts 8:12-39 and 9:10-19 for examples of hearts God has prepared.

CHAPTER 6

Witnessing to the Separated Life

"Ros, I've already witnessed to all the girls on this wing of the dorm!" Jan was as pleased to tell me as I was to hear it. She was a freshman in a State College, and she had done a great deal of praying about coming to college, because she didn't want to "lose her faith." She sincerely wanted to help others find her Saviour.

"What did you tell them?" I asked.

"They all know exactly where I stand in regard to worldly things. I told them I don't dance. I don't play cards. I don't go to shows, and I don't wear lipstick and I don't smoke! They all know I'm different and that I'm a Christian."

I waited a moment — thinking both of her desire and of their need.

"Well, Jan, I suppose they all now want to be like you?"

She gasped and a blank look came to her face.

"You don't really want them to be like *you*, do you? You want them to be like Jesus Christ, don't you?"

"Ros, I never thought of it that way! I *was* talking about myself, wasn't I? Oh, what'll I do now?"

We both thought a moment. Finally I said, "Well, one thing you could do, is to go out and buy some lipstick, then go into the dressing room with them and ask their help to put it on. And while you're there, just hope and pray someone says, 'Why, Jan, I thought you didn't wear lipstick!' Then you might say, 'Lipstick is beside the point. What I said to you girls the other day about the things I *don't* do, is *not* the point. I've begun to think about what I really *do* believe. I'm sorry about all that negative-attitude stuff. That isn't Christianity. Really it isn't. Christianity is Jesus Christ and I've suddenly discovered outward things aren't nearly as important as inward things. Belonging to Christ is what counts. I want you girls to understand.'"

Jan hid her face in her hands. "I could never do that! But what will I do?" We agreed she should keep her heart open and let God show her what to do.

Several months later, we again met, and with a sigh of relief Jan said, "What a struggle I've had. My being a Christian was all 'do this or don't do that.' Keeping rules and trying to measure up to what others thought I should do. And although I have accepted Christ as my Saviour, I nevertheless pushed Him aside in my busy attempts to make people over! I now realize that giving a witness means having Jesus Christ at the center of my desire to serve Him. Only then can I really talk about Him and not about things or myself."

Jan was fortunate to have found out so early the difference between giving a testimony and being a witness to Jesus Christ.

Most people do either one of two things when they "witness." They either give their personal testimony, or they explain why and how a person can be saved. I've heard people do both and seldom mention Jesus Christ except incidentally, like a phrase thrown in. They seem intent upon saying, even insisting, that they are different. Yet, is the non-Christian really interested in "being different" in the way you're different?

Is it any wonder your non-Christian friend may have difficulty in sorting out what is important in being a Christian? He looks at you and what does he see? What is he aware of about you? What kind of an impression are you giving him? Your silent impression often carries more positive weight than all you may say.

Sometimes I hear intelligent young people pray, "Lord, let my non-Christian friends see something different in me." And they define this "difference" as being apart and separated from worldly things. (You name them!)

Is this "being apart," this "being different" really that which attracts your friends to Jesus? Is that your testimony of how you have changed since Christ entered your life? Or is there something else?

It is absolutely imperative that we begin to look at ourselves and our conduct — and our words — through the eyes of the non-Christian. We must strive to understand his viewpoint, and begin from there. By this I in no way imply that I set aside *my* viewpoint. I do not. Rather I seek through empathy to put myself in his place. To gain his perspective and so better understand his thinking.   Only then can I hope to reach him where he has already been awakened by the Spirit of God.

The non-Christian is not attracted to Jesus nor to you by the fact that you are "different." Even your testimony does not particularly interest him. It happened to you, so what? In all probability, he is content with his life as it is now. He doesn't want to be different. At least, he doesn't want to be like most Christians he has seen!

What does attract your non-Christian friend? Briefly, the quiet confidence born of truth. Security born of faith in God. Peace born as the gift of His love and the courage to live and face life. These, expressed in daily actions, will speak far more eloquently to your non-Christian friends than most of your words.

Has anyone taken time to listen to your friend? To find out what depressed him? Where he is in his thinking? Has anyone bothered to ask him what *he* thinks about Jesus and then listened to his reply without trying to preach, interrupt, or push him too fast? Probably not. It is more likely someone testified to him, emphasized that they were "different," added to his confusion, and fostered his further rebellion. This being done in all sincerity, blind sincerity, sterile sincerity — devoid of real love. I've met these people, and so have you. Becoming a Christian is a matter of belief first and conduct later. Faith centers in a person, not a code of conduct. That Person is Jesus Christ our Lord, "the only begotten Son of God; begotten of His Father before all worlds, God of God, Light of Light, Very God of very God; Begotten not made; Being of one substance with the Father: by whom all things are made" (Common Prayer, p. 16. *Nicene Creed*).

Jesus has asked us to be witnesses to Himself, and He does not leave us to our own devices and ways. He comes to live within us, so that with His Presence we may have access to all of His wisdom, love, kindness, gentleness, and patience. He is the Good Shepherd, who loves His own and seeks the lost and troubled ones. And He seeks them and loves them, and we can reflect this love. His voice *is* speaking. When we get quiet enough, and free enough from our fears and dogmatic concepts, He will show us how to help. Show us what it means to win men by love, to faith in Himself.

Terry was a young woman working for the Social Service

Department in her state. Her main difficulty in making a decision for Christ was that she couldn't give up her worldly ways. When she saw that the decision was not between Christ and the world, but between saying *yes* or *no* to Christ, she gladly affirmed her belief in Him and invited Him into her heart.

Belief in Jesus Christ *does* raise moral issues. This, the person seeking to become a Christian must face and understand. However, our first task is to introduce them to Christ as a Person. To help them to know what He is like. Then Jesus will motivate their hearts and their wills so they'll want to acknowledge Him as Lord and Saviour.

The problem of conformity is ever with the sincere Christian. But it is not a problem which should be emphasized with a searching friend. Let's not confuse the issue for him, but let's be witnesses to Jesus Christ with a clear and simple presentation.

When it comes to new believers, we should leave the maturing process to God. We must not try to force or hurry them from our own experiences. Do you trust God enough to leave your friends in His hands? Can you see them fail a time or two, yet stand by in love and patience? If so, you too can learn from what God teaches them. His ways are higher than our ways. And no man teaches like Him.

————

Questions for thought or discussion:
1. What attracts the non-Christian?
2. What kind of an unconscious witness are your friends getting from your life?
3. Explain how outward conformity can confuse the real issue. What is the real issue?
4. Discuss the ways and means by which you can help your non-Christian friend be aware of the importance of having a Faith of his own to live by.
5. Choosing your words carefully, write a paragraph on this one idea: Why Jesus Christ is the center of my Faith. Find some friend who will listen to you while you try (without using the paper) to tell him why you believe in the Person of Jesus Christ.

CHAPTER 7

Witnessing to the Plan of Salvation

One Sunday I saw two men on the steps of a well-known Chicago church. One of them held an open Bible and was wagging his finger in the other's face. His "victim" was walking backwards down the steps.

I felt a bit ashamed — ashamed that I was identified with such a tactless Christian brother. Why didn't he invite that retreating man to a cup of coffee around the corner? Why didn't he sit down and talk with him? Why didn't he first take time to find out *why* that man had even bothered to come to church? Had he found out if there was any kind of pressing need in his life? Had he found out *where* that man was, mentally speaking, in his thinking about God?

I watched and listened for a moment, unable to take my eyes off them. Other people were watching too. The one walking backward, the other pushing forward, still wagging his finger and quoting well-known verses on the subject of salvation.

I finally walked away, praying for both of them. But I thought to myself, "I'll bet that Christian brother will be pretty elated over the good 'witness' he made today after church. He'll probably feel good the rest of the day."

And I wondered about the other man. No doubt he was glad to get away from the good brother who was pushing him so volubly.

To sensitive Christians, an experience like this leads to nameless dread and fear. Fear that they have said the wrong things. Fear that they did more harm than good. Fear that they used the wrong verses or the wrong approach. Along with this fear of hindering God's work, they pray hopefully that God will "honor His Word," at the same time hoping it will be a long time before their next opportunity to witness.

Are you one of the many hopefully wishing you had more training to aid in your desire to win others to Jesus Christ?

31

Do you wistfully sigh and think, "If only I could get into a good class on personal evangelism!"?

You can win others to Christ, with confidence and with quietness. There may be some things you have to unlearn, and some things you have to learn. But with God's help you can do both.

First of all — did that Christian on the church steps really make a witness to Christ? Do you think he did? Is giving someone verses on salvation the same as a witness to Christ? What is the difference between preaching, witnessing and testifying? At what point do you consider you have actually witnessed?

Can you evaluate a situation after it has taken place? Do you judge a good witnessing situation by how *you* feel after it is over? Or by how the other person acted? Or by the fact that you did most of the talking?

Too many people think that the only way to witness effectively is to give the plan of salvation with all the Bible verses.

Often when I speak to a group of young people, we start off with a discussion: What does it mean to witness to Jesus Christ? Invariably, I get the same answers. (1) You tell them how *you* are saved, or (2) you tell them how *they* can be saved. Or that they need to be and ought to be. When I push this a bit further, asking them exactly how they express it, I usually get an outline something like this:

1. Every man is a sinner. Romans 3:23
2. The result of sin is death. Romans 6:23
3. But God loves the sinner. Romans 5:8
4. In Christ we have deliverance. John 3:36
5. By believing in and receiving Christ we become God's children. John 1:12

I don't consider this outline to be a "witness for Christ." It is one of the many ways *to accept* the salvation which Christ offers. It is fine for one who wants to be a Christian. Countless numbers of people have found Christ through it.

But what about the man on the church steps who wants to get away as soon as possible? Shall our approach be dispensed like some patent medicine — a quick cure-all for sinners — out of the same bottle?

How is failure or success to be measured? How can we learn from our mistakes? How can we prepare our hearts, so that God can teach us to be wise, skillful, patient, loving "fishers of men"?

God help us, and the man on the church steps, when we treat people as "cases" and try to "help" them, by "doing them good." Jesus loved every single man, woman and child who came to Him, and He met their need. Their personal need. More than that, to each who came, He gave something more: a personal faith in Himself.

Instead of giving that stranger a "one-shot-preaching-session" on those church steps what might that Christian have done? How could he have approached that stranger?

1. *With a sincere regard for him as a person.* Jesus never humiliated people in public nor in private, and He never made a spectacle of Himself. Good manners and an awareness of people's feelings play a large part in an effective witness.

2. *By making the atmosphere friendly and relaxed.* We've already suggested a cup of coffee: This would have removed the strain. An audience is a subtle prod to self-effort and ego for the Christian, and a goldfish bowl for the cornered non-Christian! Then with quiet sensitivity, the Christian brother could draw the stranger he had met in church into a meaningful conversation. Personal talk about personal faith should be done with humility in a personal atmosphere — never with a third party present.

3. *He will seek to speak to the listener's need* and not to his sins. Jesus usually asked the person coming to Him, "What do you want Me to do for you?" His first need, obviously to get into Jesus' presence, being already met. His next need being his own personal problem. We must strive quietly to project our knowledge of Jesus' presence and love. We must pray for the gift of sensitivity — the eyes to see and a heart to care.

4. *By daily preparation he will be ready to have Jesus Christ walk right into the conversation,* without strain and without effort. For this is what Jesus is waiting to do. Refrain from telling him he is a sinner; God will tell him, for this is between himself and God. You tell him that God knows all about him and loves him. For it is God's love which opens hearts — not sin. Remember Jesus' words, "I, if I be lifted up, will draw all men unto me." The heart of our message is Jesus Christ —

who He is and what He can do — for all who place their trust and belief in Him.

5. *He will seek God's guidance* in determining where the Holy Spirit is already at work in the person's life. He will seek to work with God and not on a tangent of his own choosing. "What do you believe about Jesus Christ?" is a good opening question. Then listen. Search for seeds already planted, and you will know where the conversation should go from there. What else does he believe? Keep asking and drawing him out and refrain from adding too much. For the moment, what *you* believe is not important — not until he asks you. And he will ask if you quietly pray and listen with purposeful intent! You will not be afraid, because you know Christ is with you and that He will be the subject of your conversation. When Jesus enters the conversation, then you become a witness unto Him.

————

For further study:

1. Answer all the questions in this chapter.
2. Discuss the difference between
   a. Treating a man as another case.
   b. Treating him as a *person* (that is, reversing the situation, as you would want someone to approach you).
3. What further lesson has this chapter given us to add to our list of important truths about witnessing?

CHAPTER 8

Love Is the First Requisite

In the first seven chapters I related a few personal experiences through which God began to show me that love is the first requisite for witnessing. Love is not something pumped up. Love is a gift of the Spirit.

Jesus said, "Love one another as I have loved you." How did He love us? He identified Himself with us. By so doing, Christ shared our earthly problems. What else does love mean? Christ cares for us; He cared enough to do something about it. Christ accepts you as you are — just as you are — because He knows what's really in your heart. And He knows what you can become through Him! This is how we are to love one another: To remember that love identifies, love cares, love accepts. There is no superiority in love. Love is a chosen act or attitude and can be consciously controlled and directed. And love is generous.

I've heard some teachers use this motive: Because people are going to hell, we ought to witness and bring them to God. Practically speaking, most Christians do not really believe this. If they did, they would act differently. Are we all quenching the Holy Spirit in our hearts when it comes to witnessing? Honestly now — do you feel any deep urge to witness to others, or to your friends? What's back of your feeling that you should, or ought to? What's behind your feeling that you can't or haven't? Or are you among the vast crowd that dare not examine your motives?

Quite frankly, my urge to witness, to speak to others about Christ, has not always been constant. It varies. It comes and goes. And almost without exception, my lack of loving concern is caused by some obstacle between the Lord and me. At such times, I seem unwilling to become involved, and I definitely lack interest. When this becomes apparent, I seek His face, humbly and honestly asking forgiveness. I then look into the

35

faces of those around me with new interest. My heart and my eyes say to them, "God loves you . . . and . . . I care about you." When the time and place are right, I know someone whose heart has been "prepared" will be there, and Jesus Christ will walk right into the conversation. This usually happens when there is a river of out-going love from my heart.

People often give me this excuse for not sharing their faith verbally with others, "I can't express myself." Really? Then perhaps what you know and have experienced is on the meager side. Or perhaps you are under some false fear of what people may think of you? Or fear giving an incorrect answer? Or you may think people aren't interested? If so, all I can say is you don't understand people. Everyone carries some secret burden. Everyone longs for inner peace. Everyone wants a quiet heart. And everyone wants love and happiness.

Everyone is as stubborn about having religion thrust down his throat as you are! The human heart wants to make its own discoveries. But sometimes it wants someone who is an expert in gentleness to help. Certainly, all of us resist anyone who claims to be an "authority" and who tells us what we must or must not do! We need freedom to believe! Freedom to live! We also need freedom to listen, to ask questions, to share and to search.

How then can you share your faith?

This is a life-time job, I admit. Finding ways and people, sharing and loving, hoping and praying.

First, you must have

A Faith to Share

Faith is the attitude we hold for a person we trust. "Have faith in God," Jesus taught His disciples. To be able to share, you must first know whom you believe. And what you believe. Sharing what you believe is witnessing. We're going to take up the content of our faith in a couple of chapters.

Second, you must know how to

Witness With Love

In order to share your faith, or to be a witness, you must not only experience God's love within yourself, you must open your heart. Then, like a river, this love will flow out of you.

"Perfect love casts out fear," wrote the apostle John. God's love can teach us — every step of the way — how to truly love others. All God requires is an open, receptive heart! Here's a summary of what it means to witness with love.

Chapter 1. God uses any sincere effort, so let's make a start.

Chapter 2. Love avoids the impersonal approach and does not require a religious vocabulary (even though it be fortified with memory verses). There is no substitute for a quiet, friendly, personal talk, away from the eyes and ears of others.

Chapter 3. Love is never intent on "making a witness" merely to relieve conscience. Out of real concern for another, Love takes time to listen. Love does not run away!

Chapter 4. Love quickly sees the heart-needs of others. Love remains at leisure from itself — sensitive and responsive to others. Love lets *God's love* come through, at any time, any place, with any person, age, or race.

Chapter 5. Love is never in a hurry. Love never pushes. Love keeps a quiet heart, ready for the Spirit's guidance. Love is patient and waits for God's timing.

Chapter 6. When Love witnesses, it does not seek to make people over, nor to dictate behavior. With quiet confidence, Love speaks of her Beloved (Christ) and of her security and her trust in Him.

Chapter 7. Love does not substitute methods for a living relationship. Love is sensitive and seeks to discern where the Spirit is already at work in another. Love does not go off on a tangent of its own.

When love speaks, God is there. When God is there (and where can one go where He is not?) it is always possible to speak in words of love. To be conscious of God's presence with us, is simply to include Him. To look to Him and to turn our minds toward Him, takes less than a split-second.

Nothing less than the goal of being totally committed to Jesus Christ (body, soul and spirit; past, present and future) will give God the wide open door He needs to live in you and to love through you. This takes time. In fact, it takes a life-time, and there's no lesser goal. But why not start now?

However, lest you be a perfectionist, or one easily discouraged by ups and downs, let me clarify:

God is faithful and He cannot deny His character even if I am unfaithful. If no instrument of "perfect love" is there, He will use an imperfect instrument. (You! Me!) Haven't you experienced this? Admit it and relax; this is *trust* in the presence of *grace*. There have been times when I haven't kept my daily devotions. Times I've been off-center on some selfish pursuit (God help me and He does!) To my utter amazement (but not to God's), someone not only crosses my path who wants to talk about Him, but who is ready to accept Christ and does!

One day, on my knees, I said to the Lord, "Why do I have to have all these ups and downs! Why hasn't that experience of 'the second blessing' given 15 years ago, taken away the ups and downs? Why haven't I been able to get on an even keel and stay there?"

His answer came immediately, "My child, if you could do everything for yourself, you wouldn't need a Saviour. You would depend only upon yourself and upon your own faith. You learn more through the *downs* than you do through the *ups*. Accept them. By doing so, you learn patience, and eventually I will transform them into meaning for you which you will understand."

You can trust Him always to do the loveliest thing possible. You need never fear Him nor His ways. And you can trust Him to show you His ways of love in being His witness.

I used to have a hazy concept of God's love for sinners. I thought He loved only those obedient to Him. And that put me "in the doghouse" much of the time. It was a wonderful day when I discovered that I, too, am still a sinner: A sinner who has been saved, who is being saved, and who will be saved! And when I began to read my Bible as a "sinner being saved," what a difference!

And what a difference it made in the way I looked at people around me. Anna Mow has a story in her book, *Say Yes to Life* (Zondervan), which illustrates what I mean. A lady living in the suburbs used to watch one of her neighbors go to work each morning while she washed her breakfast dishes. She had invited him to church many times and given him religious tracts. Often, as she watched him, she said to herself, "There goes a man without God." Then she began to be aware that God's love is extended to all, that Christ died for all (Romans 5:8; II Corinthians 5:15). One morning watching her neighbor leave for work, the truth broke through! She found herself saying, "There goes a man whom God loves!"

Why don't you try it?

Fear is based on the unknown; on what we think may happen. Love casts out fear. Love is the heart's song of freedom. We only know freedom when our heart is safely at rest within the heart of God and that of our Lord and Saviour, Jesus Christ.

Love opens the door that enables us to witness for God joyfully and without fear.

For you today:
1. Give love to everyone whom you meet today, through your heart and your eyes. Let each conscious look into another's eyes be God's love coming through you to them.
2. Pray for and be ready for a conversation with someone today, where you can speak with love, acceptance and caring.

PART II

Love
Is
Willing
to
Be
Involved

CHAPTER 9

What Is a Witness?

A witness to Jesus Christ is one who knows Him and is interested in introducing Him to others.

You may not like to be called an "evangelist" but the meaning of the Greek word is one who tells forth what he knows to be Truth, regarding both the facts of his belief, as well as his own personal experience. This means our testimony must be both in deed and in word. The spoken word is never really effective unless it is backed up by the life. The living deed is ultimately inadequate without the spoken word. The reason for this is obvious. No life is good enough to speak by itself. Any person who says, "I don't need to witness; I just let my life speak," is unbearably self-righteous.

Since communication of important convictions and beliefs is impossible without language, we must witness verbally. In an early edition of *Creating Christian Cells,* Samuel Shoemaker says, "I cannot by being good, tell of Jesus' atoning death and resurrection, nor of my faith in His divinity. The emphasis is too much on me and too little on Him."

The early Christians suffered terribly because of their faith, but like some Christians today, they believed that faith which is not shared is not genuine. If members of churches who think themselves correct in their theology would match the zeal of certain sects (who give at least 60 hours a month to witnessing and house-to-house visitation) a book on witnessing would not be necessary.

Is anyone still trying to hide behind the threadbare excuse that witnessing is for those with special gifts and special training? We are all involved. To each of us comes this call: "Come follow me! Ye shall be witnesses unto me!" Each Christian has a story worth telling, and an opportunity to approach another person in a unique way.

We need to face our fears. Writing them down helps us see

how flimsy they are. Reading good books helps us find the areas of belief and approach which most of us already know, but have forgotten. We need freshness in our approach. We need love for our fellow-man. We need to know that we are witnesses to Christ, not to theology, and that we are presenting a Person, not a set of rules.

Our Personal Preparation

You must know a person before you can introduce him to someone else. This is why Jesus said that we will be powerful witnesses for Him, when the Holy Spirit has come into our hearts (Acts 1:8). People used to confuse me when they asked, "Have you received your baptism?" Now I know I was baptized by the Holy Spirit into Christ when I opened my heart for Christ to enter (I Corinthians 12:13). There is one baptism but many fillings of the Holy Spirit. His new life in me brought changes of outlook, of purpose and of relationship. Christ became real to me, and His love is more than adequate for all of my failures and life's futilities.

We are witnesses of the above facts, because they happened to us. But we must be verbal witnesses primarily to Christ, not to our changed lives. Our changed lives should be silent witnesses to Christ's power. These aspects of witnessing will be discussed in the next chapter. As the Holy Spirit within us is our teacher, our knowledge of Christ grows and our knowledge of ourselves and others matures. We need the Holy Spirit within us to know *when* to approach another, what subject to start with, how far to go, when to urge a bit, and when to allow time for thinking. The spirit within us is Christ in us, guiding us (II Corinthians 3:17, 18).

The reason we do not have confidence when we witness to our faith, is that we think it's up to us. It is never up to us! When we make this plain, the other party is relieved, and so are we! Then God can get on with His own persuading without having us get in His way.

We must be willing to accept involvement with others. Jesus became involved to the point of being rejected, falsely accused and crucified — for our sakes. His call comes to us today. "Be willing for involvement with me — with others. For my sake, for their sake, for love's sake!"

He bore witness to Truth: "I am the Way, the Truth and the

Life." We bear witness to Him, who is the Truth, and to the effect He has on our lives.

Our Message

I vividly remember the first time I fully realized Christ Himself is the center of our message, *not* something about Him.

It was in a booth at the Jolly Joan Cafe in Portland, Oregon. Eugene Thomas, my friend and fellow-worker from Colorado, sat across from me. His own conversion to Christ had come through no verbal witness, but through devouring one book after another until he was convinced that belief in Jesus Christ is the touchstone of personal Christianity. Gene's own life is characterized by this initial simplicity. I had all the trappings of 18 years of organized Christianity still strapped on me, even though I'd broken through quite a few by that time.

"Jesus Christ! He is the one we must talk about, study about, think about. Jesus Christ: *Who He really is,* first of all, and then what He did, and why. Jesus Christ was God in the flesh! If not, what He did on the cross is of no value at all."

Sitting across from me, Gene continued his enthusiastic single-track conversation. I listened. He was right. Of course he was right! What *had* I been emphasizing in my work as a student-counselor for five years? First one thing, then another, but where was the center?

The light of the character of Christ shone from Gene's rugged face. With elbows on the table, chin cupped in hands, his broad smile and relaxed attitude confirmed his words. "Jesus Christ is the center of our message! Christianity *is* Christ."

Gene was right. At that moment, it seemed as though no one had ever before nailed it down in such words. I had gone through periods when teaching on the atonement, and Holy Spirit, were central, but what about Christ? Had I left Him out in my eagerness to understand and share His Gospel?

Jesus Christ is our message to the world. To the degree that we know Him and are able to communicate Him to others, so that they may know in whom to believe, in this measure only are we mature witnesses.

After Gene returned to Colorado, the thought he had planted in my mind, kept growing. I began to relate all I knew about the Christian faith to one thing: to the Person of Christ.

To what had I been witnessing? Primarily to the fact that

one is not alive spiritually until he is born of the Spirit; that this birth of the Spirit is possible only through the atonement Jesus made possible by His death and resurrection. I was witnessing to the new birth!

Now I began to see. The central message of Christianity is Christ, who He is, what He has done, and what He can and will do. The central message of Christianity is not: "If you will accept Jesus Christ as your Saviour who died on the Cross because He loved you, and give up your old life, you can be saved." The central message of Christianity is: "What are you waiting for? Believe now in the Person of the Lord Jesus Christ. Everything is finished! He has already taken care of your sins! This is the very essence of the Crucifixion and the Resurrection."

Both are true. The first places the responsibility on your choice and the Cross. The second assures you that belief in Christ, the living Lord, takes care of you and your new life.

How can men call on Him in whom they have not believed? And how shall they believe in Him of whom they have never heard? And how shall they hear unless someone tells them?

To be a witness to Jesus Christ! The whole subject became intensely interesting. I had to know more about Him. My Bible became a new book for me. It became a source book for the life and teachings of Jesus, instead of a place to secure proof-texts for what I believed. I found new joy in searching out the human and the divine characteristics of Jesus, as I watched Him walk through the pages of the New Testament. Even the epistles took on a new glow, as I saw the centrality of the fact that Jesus was God in the flesh.

As I began sharing these truths with my students, I realized one of the major problems of belief in Christ today, is confusion as to His identity. Their question: How can Jesus be God when He is the Son of God? My question: How can anyone believe in Him, when they don't know who He is?

From these new insights came the material for my study book on the Gospel of Mark, *Who Is This Man?* Together, students could discover the identity of Jesus as they read about Him, and noted His claims and His deeds. For knowing *about Him,* is the first step in coming *to know Him.*

A witness to Jesus Christ is one who knows Him, and who is able to communicate this knowledge to others, so they too may know Him.

For your consideration:

1. Define: witness. Your preparation. Your message.
2. What was the main subject about which the early church bore witness? Acts 1:21; 2:24, 32; 3:15; 4:10; 5:30-32.
3. Do you possess one of the recently published New Testaments in modern English? By all means secure at least one for yourself and one to lend to a friend.

FOR GENERAL READING:

The Berkeley Version (Zondervan, Grand Rapids)
The Revised Standard Version (Thomas Nelson & Sons, N.Y.)
The New English Bible-New Testament (Cambridge & Oxford)

FOR HELP IN STUDY:

The Amplified New Testament (Zondervan)
The New Testament (an expanded translation) Wuest (Eerdman's, Grand Rapids)

FOR SIMPLIFIED READING:

Norlie's Simplified New Testament (Zondervan)
20th Century New Testament (Moody)
The New Testament in the Language of the People, Williams (Moody)

FOR PROVOCATIVE READING:

New Testament in Modern English, J. B. Phillips (Macmillan)

CHAPTER 10

The Psychology of Making a Witness

Recently I heard a definition of evangelism which delighted me. "Evangelism is one beggar telling another beggar where to find bread." (Dr. D. T. Niles) So we are back again to you and to me, and now we are both beggars! One cannot be a beggar standing on a "holier than thou" pedestal. Even the beggar who finds bread, knows his discovery has not changed his class status; but it has filled his stomach — hunger ceases and relaxed satisfaction sets in.

Are you taking your place as a "sinner *being* saved" along with the rest of the sinners? If so, others will listen to you. If not, you've already lost your audience. Check your own attitude and tone of value. Try to remember you are the beggar who has found the Bread. "I am the Bread of life," said Jesus in John 6. "He who comes to me shall not hunger, and he who believes in me shall never thirst." Remember there are other beggars looking for bread! You'd tell them where to find it, wouldn't you? And how you tell a person about spiritual satisfaction is just as important as telling them where to find it.

We have defined a witness as one who knows the truth concerning Christ and is able to share that truth as it concerns his daily life. This may be defined as *an objective witness* and a *subjective witness.* An objective witness points to Christ — His claims, His Person, His cross; a subjective witness points to self and tells what God has done in your life. In this chapter we're going to explore both these areas, including strategy, asking questions, and the use of intrigue in the initial approach.

The objective approach deals with an external subject, and the subjective approach with an internal one. The objective deals with Jesus Christ. The subjective approach pertains to one's own feelings, emotions and inner self. What you think about Christ has to be objective and can lead one to a good

48

conversation; while the question, "Do you want to be a Christian?" is very subjective and can lead either to self-defense or to decision.

The Subjective Approach

Most people call this "giving a personal testimony." A personal testimony is an important art of witnessing, and the confidence with which you speak of what God has done for you, will count far more than the actual story you tell. You can't share what you don't have. Answers don't grow on trees, and notebooks don't have loudspeakers to dispense information. Only as we daily work out life's answers, can we gain insight into the needs of others.

When you tell a story of God's working in your life, you must be aware of the difference between giving a mature or an immature witness. An immature witness bubbles out, spills out, runs over, full of generalities related by a person intoxicated with his own experience. A mature witness will not bore others with generalities, but will be specific and only share what the other person needs. In mature witnessing, concentration is not on what you say, but on getting the other person and the Lord together. You are concerned with where they are and where they ought to be. Just as Jesus was.

While Anna Mow was in India, she was asked, "Have you given your witness to Mrs. Pundit?" Anna felt it her business to be Mrs. Pundit's friend, not to thrust her witness down her throat! One afternoon, four years later, Mrs. Pundit opened her heart and talked all afternoon. Maturity brings wisdom to know whether our reluctance is a lack of courage, or the check of the Spirit to await God's time.

It was when a neighbor whose teenager had problems, asked, "What's happened to your Tom?" that Marie recognized an open door. She could now share the almost miraculous answer to prayer she and Nick had experienced in regard to their teenage son. But with another friend, she had to resort to a question in order to tell her story, "Louise, have you noticed the change in Tom?"

Arousing interest through intrigue is an art. It can be done in many ways, but I'd like to suggest one which has worked for me. It's the art of asking questions, which is much more apt to arouse the interest of the listener than "preaching." In fact, preaching is not witnessing. When you start to preach, you are telling the other person what to do, and the first thing you know, you've become a judge. And a judge is not a witness. When you judge anyone, you make him feel guilty. People only feel real guilt before God. But if *you* make them feel guilt, it will be a false-guilt causing them to avoid you and God, and the next person who tries to witness to them will have an even more difficult time.

What kind of witness are you? Someone has said, "Christianity is not taught — it's caught."

When you have a story to tell about how you learned to love someone you disliked, or how God took the jealousy out of your heart, or how resentment turned to forgiveness, or how your marriage was saved — here are a few points for effective witness. They were given at a Faith at Work Conference, by Rev. Lionel A. Whiston, of Wrentham, Mass.

"Tell it in story form, with all the characteristics of drama: contrast, suspense, vividness, punchline and climax. The story carries its own witness and power — there is no need to preach, or to drive it home, or to exhort! It tells what God has done. It gives credit and glory to God. It's personal. It's fresh in time and in spirit. It speaks to the listener's need, not to his sins. It does not destroy faith, it builds faith. It's in intelligible and pungent English. It's alive and enthusiastic. It's always in good taste. It's brief. It includes encounter with God and with man."

The person to whom you witnessed will probably have one of three reactions. You should be prepared for them and know what to do next.

First. *Indifference.* "So what, it happened to you, but I don't want it to happen to me. I'm not interested." (This person is obviously not ready to hear more, and don't antagonize him by trying. Let him know you respect his freedom of thought.)

Second. *Negative.* "I couldn't be less interested! I don't believe in religion. Everyone is a hypocrite and there aren't any true Christians." (A blast like this is encouraging, because it means someone has "rubbed him the wrong way." Ask him about it. Let him get it out of his system and be understanding. He'll probably be willing to get on the positive side.)

Third. *Positive.* "Well — that's interesting. (silence) I don't think I ever heard anyone be quite that honest before." Here it's time to go into some phase of the Objective Approach.

The Objective Approach

A good question helps us find where the other person is in his thinking about Christ. Let's say we've had a negative answer from someone, "I don't want to be like the Christians I've seen." Immediately agree by saying, "I don't either, that's why I've come to the conclusion that all Christians are sinners *being* saved. But the important question for *you* to ask yourself is, '*What do you think about Jesus Christ?*' "

"What do I think about Christ?" repeated an intelligent young man. "Well, I don't believe in Him. I believe in God . . . but not in a personal God. I don't believe Jesus was God. He was a good man and a great teacher."

We were off to a good start. Quietly I said, "Well, you probably know that I believe Jesus was God in the flesh and my belief is based on His claims as well as His deeds." (I was using intrigue in my approach, and it had the desired effect.)

"What do you mean? What did He claim?"

From here we went into the Gospel of John and read Jesus' own words — "Who is the man?" (5:12) "My Father is working and I am working. This was why the Jews sought all the more to kill him, because he not only broke the Sabbath, but also called God his Father, making himself equal with God" (John 5:17, 18). Who do you claim to be? (John 10:30-33; John 14:8-11). We looked at these claims Christ made and the young man admitted he had not, as an adult, read the New Testament. He wanted to read it. I suggested a few of the many fine modern translations on the market, and he wrote them down.

I did not urge a decision . . . in any way, shape, or form. When he reads the New Testament (not in Shakespearean English, but in easily understood modern English) he will be personally examining the claims of Christ to deity. And the interesting fact is the tables will turn and soon the One whom he is examining will be examining him!

Did you notice, I completely ignored the first words the young man spoke, about Christ being a good man and a great teacher? I led him into the claims of Christ. When he reads these, he either has to accept them "because Christ is a good man and a great teacher" or reject them, because He is not. Sometimes I do discuss this subject, but there is no set rule.

In the Objective Approach there are several questions which can be used as a catalyst or a stimulant to begin a meaningful conversation.

1. I, personally, like these the most: What do you think of Christ? Or what do you believe about Christ? These were illustrated in the story just told.

2. A friend of mine finds this works for him: "Are you a believer in Christ yet? Or, are you still on the way?" The answer could be, "Well, I guess I'm still on the way." Your next question: "How far along are you?" "When did you get started?" Your aim being to show that Christ Himself is the way. John 14:6.

3. Another friend uses this set of questions: "Are you interested in spiritual things?" "Are you interested in being a real Christian?" "What do you think a real Christian is?" A young woman asked her landlord these questions one night while he was fixing her radiator. Yes, he was interested in spiritual things. No, he'd never even *seen* a real Christian! Her answer surprised him: "Well, look at me, I'm a sincere Christian." From this, they entered into a real and animated Christ-centered discussion.

The goal of the objective approach is to present Christ. Immanuel — God with us (Isaiah 9:6, 7). There are two subjects of primary importance: Who Christ is, and why He came. Theology calls these the Atonement and the Incarnation. You should study these until you are able to give either a brief explanation or a detailed one. Every witness will contain something about one or both of these subjects. Learning more about presenting these in conversational and easily comprehended English will be discussed in the next two chapters.

––––––––––

For discussion and thought:

1. What is the word mentioned in this chapter, which, when properly handled, results in interest being kindled?
2. Since it is a psychological fact that _____ (same word as above) and interest are the doors to personal discovery, how can you share your faith, yet let the other person feel he is making the discovery himself?
3. What is the difference between an immature and a mature witness?

4. Explain the goal and the subject matter in giving an objective or subjective witness.
5. Name three possible reactions a person could have to your witness: why they reacted as they did, and what your next move should be.
6. How was intrigue used in the conversation with the young man in this story? Read the story in chapter 13 for an example of how intrigue was used in talking to a stranger.

CHAPTER 11

Sharing Knowledge of Christ's Claims

In the last chapter the word *witness* was defined as: one who knows both the facts and the truth concerning the Person of Jesus Christ and who can share this knowledge with others.

What did the early disciples talk about when they witnessed? Have you ever studied the actual message preached by the young church? Their emphasis was not that men had sinned, or that they were different, or even on their personal experience. The central message was that Jesus whom they knew, and who had taught and healed among them, was God's Chosen One! God had made Himself personally known through Jesus. This Jesus was God's Christ. *The resurrection of Jesus Christ from the dead!* The heart of their message was: "This Jesus, God has made both Lord and Christ!" (Acts 2:36).

What does it mean for us to witness to Jesus Christ today? Is His *resurrection* news? It was news at that time, because everyone knew that Jesus, the great Teacher, had been crucified. What is news today? The greatest religious news today is that God did visit this planet in the Person of Jesus of Nazareth. Without Jesus Christ we would not know the God Christians worship. He is the God who is always with us and in us, through His Holy Spirit. How do we know? How can we tell others?

How can you witness to the Person of Christ?

From the knowledge you possess right now concerning the *life of Jesus* (not His death), how long do you think you could talk about Him to someone who doesn't know Him without mentioning His cross or His death? What could you tell of Jesus, and about Jesus, that would make a non-Christian feel Jesus loves him and might be interested in him, too? Try it

sometime, with a friend, and time yourself. You may be in for
a surprise.

In many of our conferences in the Pacific Northwest, and in
California, we tried role-playing with our students in an effort
to sharpen their incentive for fresh learning in coming workshops.

We asked for two volunteers, one to play the role of a non-
Christian, interested but not antagonistic; and one to be a wit-
nessing Christian talking to him about the Person of Christ.
But not the death of Christ. This was to come later.

I recall two young men who thought this would be an easy
assignment. They sat in two chairs before the class, and to start
them off we gave them an opening line. In less than a minute,
they had nothing to say. The "witnessing" Christian found all he
could say, was, "Why, it's easy to believe in Jesus Christ. Why,
you just believe . . . believe . . . believe on *Him*. Just *believe*."

"Believe what?" the other asked.

And because we had previously stated our conditions . . .
they didn't know what else to say about Him!

To believe is not the only difficulty. To discover what to
believe is the major difficulty, in a day when Christendom is
full of "Christianities," which not only do not agree, but exclude
one another. What are we to believe about Jesus Christ? In
all this confusion, the Voice of Jesus comes to us afresh, speaking from Caesarea Philippi to bring us to the point of importance:

"Who are men saying that I am?"

"What do you say of me? Who do you say that I am?" Jesus
turns to His disciples for their answer.

For an instant, like the sun shining through the bright-dark
clouds, the Truth came to Peter. He lost the brightness for a
time, but He never really lost the Truth.

"You are the Christ, the Son of the living God." And because
the time was not yet ripe for the disclosure, He told them to tell
no one.

After almost three years of being with Him, watching Him,
listening to Him, had He given them enough clues to His identity? He apparently thought He had, although He knew their
minds were still clouded.

Here is a question for some discussion: When did the disciples

really know who Jesus was? The answer: Not until after the
Resurrection did they fully know He was God in the flesh, Immanuel, God with us.

What claims did Jesus make for Himself?

There were the unspoken claims to His oneness with His
Father in the physical healings of incurable disease as well as
mental illness. The blind were given sight, the lame walked,
the deaf heard, lepers were cleansed, the dead raised to life
again. "Son, your faith has made you whole." "Daughter, go
in peace, your faith in me has made you well."

There is an unmistakable tone of authority in all He taught
them about Himself. Other religious leaders taught truth, He
said, "I am the Truth." He made Himself the center of His
message. They said, "Come, we will show you the way." Jesus
said, "I am the Way." Others were lost, He is the Shepherd.
Others were ill, He is the Physician. Others were sinners, He is
the Saviour. Were any thirsty? "Come unto me and drink."
Were they hungry with any kind of hunger? "I am the Bread
of Life, he who comes to me shall not hunger, and he who
believes in me, shall never thirst." Were any weary ones seeking shelter? "Come unto me and rest. I am the door, if any
one enters by me, he will be saved, and will go in and out and
find pasture."

What was Jesus like?

Jesus came to introduce a new way of life and of love into a
troubled Roman world where men were bought, sold and tor-
tured as slaves. His readiness to give time and attention to unim-
portant people puzzled and bewildered the race- and class-
conscious world of that day.

"He was tender to the unfortunate, patient with honest inquir-
ers. But He insulted respectable clergymen by calling them
hypocrites. He referred to King Herod as 'that fox' and He
went to parties in disreputable company. He was looked upon
as a gluttonous man and a wine-bibber, a friend of publicans
and sinners. He assaulted indignant tradesmen and threw
them and their belongings out of the Temple; He drove a coach-
and-horses through a number of sacrosanct . . . regulations.

"He had a courage and sureness about Him that made those
who came to spy on Him, go away saying, 'No man ever talked

as He does.' When confronted with neat doctrinal questions, he showed a kind of humor that affronted the ruling religious party and he answered them by disagreeable searching questions that could not be answered by any rule of thumb."[1]

What does the Church think of Christ?

The church believes that Jesus of Nazareth, was in fact and in truth, and in the most exact and literal sense of the words, the "God by whom all things are made."[2] He was both God and man, as far as the personality of God could be expressed in human terms. He was not merely a man so good as to be "like God" — *He was God.*

"We believe that Jesus Christ is God and Man. Perfect God and perfect Man, of a reasonable soul and human flesh subsisting. Who although He be God and Man, yet is He not two, but one Christ." (Westminster Catechism).

Know More About Jesus Christ

Identify yourself with just one character from one of the New Testament healings. Take for instance the blind man, Bartimaeus. Think through what his life must have been like, where he heard about Jesus, his hopes, his fears, what he heard and from whom, how he knew Jesus was in that crowd, what was said and done. And what you, as the blind man healed, would have talked about for hours and weeks and months after that. How much more knowledge about the Man who healed you would you have accumulated? Would you have any difficulty talking about Him, if you had been Bartimaeus?

Would you still excuse yourself by saying "I can't express myself"? Could you put this kind of interest, love, enthusiasm and convincing faith regarding the Person of Jesus, across to your non-Christian friend today? If not, why not? Others are learning. You can too. But you must take long, long looks at Jesus. You must read carefully what He did. You must understand the hopelessness of each person devoid of Christ. You must also read carefully and thoughtfully what Jesus said about Himself.

[1]Dorothy Sayers, *The Greatest Drama Ever Staged* (Hodder & Stoughton)
[2]Hebrews 1, Colossians 1, John 1.

It will not be by your efforts alone, that the revelation of who Jesus is, will come to your friend. Pray that the heart of your friend shall be open to God's Spirit, who does the revealing, the showing, the final convincing. Read the invitation given in Matthew 11:28-30, "Come unto me," and then read the whole eleventh chapter and see how many knew who He was. Then read verses 25-27 and see what Jesus said about who can understand this truth.

"Come to Me," Jesus says. "Learn of Me, and you will find rest for your souls." Learn about me, who I am, what I am like, that I accept you as you are, that I care about you, that I love you, that I want you to belong to me. Learn that I am your Good Shepherd, and that you need not walk alone. The Good Shepherd gives His life for the sheep. Every one whom the Father has given me will come to me. "For this is my Father's will, that everyone who sees the Son and believes in Him shall have eternal life, and I will raise him up at the last day."

When Philip said, "Lord, show us the Father, and we will be satisfied," Jesus' reply was, "How long have I been with you without your recognizing Me, Philip! He who has looked on Me has looked on the Father. What do you mean by saying, show us the Father? Do you not believe that I am in the Father and the Father in Me?" (John 14:8-10).

The only way to be able to put your trust in any person, is to know that person, and know what he is like. When we emphasize personal salvation more than a Personal Saviour, we are asking people to put their trust in an experience rather than in Jesus Christ.

"In the beginning was the Word, and the Word was with God, and the Word was God. He Himself was in the beginning with God. Through Him everything came into being and without Him nothing that exists came into being. In Him was Life, and the Life was the Light of men . . . And the Word became flesh and tented among us, and we viewed His glory — abounding in grace and truth."

Jesus is still asking:

What do you say of Me?

What is your attitude about Me?

Questions for thought and discussion:

1. Read the following scriptures and notice that it is *who* we believe in, not *what*. All from John's Gospel: 3:16, 36; 6:35, 40; 8:25-30; 9:35-38; 11:25-27.
2. What was the main subject to which Christians of the early church were eye-witness? All from the Acts of the Apostles: 1:21; 2:24, 32; 3:15; 4:10; 5:30-32; 10:39-43.
3. When *you* witness, what is your main subject?
4. How does one witness to the (resurrection) living Christ today?

CHAPTER 12

Sharing Faith in Christ's Cross

In the film, *Ben Hur*, the blood of Christ ran red from the cross. Only His feet were shown, nailed to the rough upright, while the flash of lightning showed His blood running red down from the cross, into the pools of rain water, into the face of the earth.

Three of my friends were profoundly influenced by this film. One, a Jewish woman, said it was one of the turning points in her faith in Christ. Another, still a seeker, said, "I could scarcely wait to see His face after I heard His voice, and saw His kindness to that prisoner; and they didn't show His face!" Loren, a very new Christian, said, "I was glad I was a Christian when I saw what happened to Jesus."

What does the cross of Christ mean to you? Can you, as His witness, share what you believe? Yes, you can. You can share your belief, as far as it goes, in a simple, clear manner. You can even share your unbelief, by saying, "I know there must be more meaning to His cross and His death, and I hope to be able to understand more some day; but for right now, this is what I see."

You *can* identify yourself with your seeking friend in this way, because if you speak as an "authority" on theological matters, you probably have already lost him. People want sureness and confidence when it comes to experience. You must think even more carefully when you speak about the Cross of Christ. You can share what you believe in your heart, when you witness, but you must avoid what your mind deduces about theology. Argument has never won a soul! Sharing and listening, questioning and listening — with heavy emphasis on listening — will help you reach your seeking friend and lead him on to where God wants him to be.

Personally, I find more people open and willing to talk from

the question, *What do you think about Jesus Christ?* than the
question, "Would you like to be saved?" And in my experience
more people accept Christ and come to new life in Him, through
knowledge of *Who He is,* rather than why He died. This seems
to come afterwards. I don't know what approach is best for
you. It will depend on your knowledge of Christ, your knowledge of human nature, and how much of God's love you are
willing to let flow from your heart to another heart.

The death and Cross of Christ is a great divider of Christians. Thanks to God, His Spirit in us, which is Life, is the
great uniter! And what a pity that the former is true. Fre-
quently one group will not accept another group unless exactly
the right terminology is used about His death. But it is not
terminology that saves us from sin, it is God's love as shown
in Christ.

I have had young people ask me, "How can I tell my friends
about Jesus' death without using Bible language?" There is
an excellent paper-backed book which tells the story for the
twentieth-century mind. *The Fact of Christ,* by P. Carnegie
Smith (published in England, available through Inter-Varsity
Christian Fellowship, Chicago), teaches fresh ways to witness to
Jesus Christ, to the fact that He is God, to His claims, to His
character, to His life and to His death.

When God Was Man, by J. B. Phillips (Abingdon) is another
small book with great truths along this line.

I have a friend in Washington, D.C. who buys Eugenia
Price's *Strictly Personal* (Zondervan) by the half-dozen to give
to interested and open-minded people.

C. S. Lewis has a strange and beautiful fantasy for children,
as well as adults, in *The Lion, The Witch and The Wardrobe*
(Harper's). There are no words for religion or salvation in this
book, yet the Truth shines forth like a great light.

The Cross of Christ

When God became man, as Jesus of Nazareth, He did so
with full knowledge of what it would mean. He identified
Himself fully and wholly with mankind. He took upon Himself
all earthly vicissitudes as well as the result of all that evil is and
does to us — in separating us from God. Since death is the
result of sin, so in His dying, Jesus took upon Himself the sin
of the whole world. By His resurrection we are assured of the

forgiveness of our sins and of life everlasting. He banished forever "the sting of death" and assures our reconciliation with God. This He did both in His life and His death, by becoming our substitute and our representative (Romans 5:10; II Corinthians 5:21). The Jewish or Old Testament explanation was accepted by Paul.

What then was Jesus' Cross and agony all about? The answer to this question is contained in the meaning of the phrase: Christ's union with us and our sin.

Sin is wanting our own way, as opposed to God's way. Anything is sin, which is not God's will for us. It may even be something we consider good. For example: Remember Jonah and the whale? It was no sin to buy a ticket on that boat sailing for Joppa. Joppa was a city like any other city. But it was a sin for Jonah, because God had clearly told him to go to Nineveh!

Jesus had no sin of His own. He was blameless and sinless. He took the sin of the world (our sins) upon Himself, and *became sin* for us. We cannot know the meaning of Jesus' death without personal pronouns. Our, us, me. They say it all. Christ died for *our* sins. He gave Himself for *me* (Galatians 2:20).

I remember hearing a Chinese preacher express it like this: "The result of sin is death. Jesus Christ would still be alive today if our *sins* had not been laid upon Him; because, having no sin of His own, death could never have touched Him. It was our *sins* that killed Him, not the nails in His hands and feet."

"The blood of Jesus Christ, His Son, cleanseth us from all sin" (I John 1:7). The blood means the life, the life of Christ, given, poured out. His life given for us, is given forever. His love given to us, is given forever.

Jesus came to reveal the heart of the Father to His lost world. He and the Father are one, and He came to make us one with Himself.

Having provided forgiveness for His estranged world, God's problem was that people were blind and could not see that they had been both forgiven and loved. *For the Lamb was slain from the foundation of the world.* With God there is no time — no past, no present, no future. Only an eternal *now*. Only eternity!

Man's continual "blindness" made it necessary for the crucified Christ, being who He is, to come into view! Into plain view. Into history.

Seeing the crucified Christ, we *know* God's forgiveness.

Seeing the resurrected Christ, we *know* it is all true. We are forgiven! We need only accept God's forgiveness: It is all there and has been all the time! This is the meaning of the Cross.

"You cannot have forgiveness," says Mr. Simpson in his book, "without having the Forgiver, without admitting Him to an inward union with your mind, and heart and life."

Only thus does Christ's own answer become our answer. Because in Himself, He answered all the conditions — having Him, we have all the answers! Following Him, and loving Him and belonging to Him, we know the Voice of our Shepherd, and shall go in and out and find pasture.

A practical suggestion:

> Try writing a letter to a friend and explain in your own words, Christ's death. Try telling a friend.

CHAPTER 13

Talking to Strangers

Question: When traveling on a train or a bus, sitting next to a stranger, how can you approach the subject of salvation?

In the first place, my subject wouldn't be "salvation." Instead it would be Jesus Christ. Initially, it's not what I say that is important. It is important that I listen and find out where the person I'm addressing has arrived in his thinking.

Every day brings to each of us a variety of experiences as we come in contact with lives destined to touch our own — even briefly. What we say and do in these brief encounters may have great impact and influence — for God does guide us in more ways than we know.

A Bus Ride

In a small Montana town I boarded the 9:00 A.M. bus bound for Spokane. There were only four people in the bus, all sitting in the front seats. I was pleased, for I had hoped to sit alone during the four-hour journey so that I might do some reading.

About a half hour later, I was a bit startled when two of the men seated up front moved to seats directly behind me. Finding the smoke from their cigars and their conversation distracting, I was moving to another seat, when an inner impulse seemed to say, "Stay where you are." Then the voice of the Spirit speaking through my heart, said, "How do you know I didn't put them right there behind you?"

I sighed and with a mental shrug of resignation remained where I was. Shortly after I'd finished my devotions and turned my attention to some other reading, one of the men got off the bus. The other man leaned over the back of my seat and began reading over my shoulder. "What are you reading, lady?" he asked.

Casually polite, I answered, "Oh, some mimeographed sheets

64

on the problems of capital and labor and how Christians should
deal with them."

"Oh, well, I figured you must have something to do with Christians," was his unexpected comment. It was rather a left-handed
introduction, but at least the subject had been mentioned.

I asked his destination, and when he replied, "Bellingham,
Washington," I mentioned that my brother, Bruce Rinker, is a
practicing attorney in that city.

"Well," he said, "it's a small world, isn't it? I know him. In
fact, when my son injured his hand, it was your brother who
helped him collect liability insurance."

We chatted a bit. He told me his name was Smith, and I
told him of my frequent visits to the college in Bellingham —
then the conversation changed.

"I'm planning on taking a course in accounting at the college,
maybe you'll make a visit while I'm there?" At this, I turned
to look at him. He was an older man, gray and slightly bald.
"You are?" I asked. "How do you plan to use this course in
accounting?"

To my astonishment and without any warning, he leaned back,
bent over, and started to cry — great sobs shook his entire body.
That an older man would display deep emotion in such a public
place as a bus could only mean one thing — a situation too big
for him, a burden too heavy for him to carry.

My heart sent up a petition to God. "What shall I do now?"
There was an immediate answer. Reaching back I gently
touched his shoulder, "Mr. Smith, I don't know what's wrong,
but Jesus does, for He loves you. He cares very much about
why you are so troubled."

As Mr. Smith straightened and reached for his handkerchief,
I moved quietly into the seat beside him. He apologized for
his sudden display of emotion. "It's just that I'm so tired, un-
happy, and upset." Then, without any attempt to conceal his
bitterness, he said, "Three days ago my wife left me. I followed
her to South Dakota, where I found her living with another
man. If I had had a gun with me I'd have killed them both!
Yes, both of them! I mean it!'

"I don't doubt you, Mr. Smith, for you are no better than
your wife."

My words startled him and he looked at me questioningly.
Continuing, I said, "She committed adultery but you wanted to

commit murder. And I'm sure you know as well as I that Jesus said the thought is as bad as the deed."

"Lady, aren't you being awfully hard on me?" he asked.

"No, Mr. Smith, I'm not; but God happens to love your wife just as much as He loves you!"

He looked at me for a long moment, and turned away as the tears came again. I leaned toward him and said quietly, "God bless you. And He will. He loves you. Try to pray, won't you? Just admit to God that you are a sinner like everyone else, and say, 'God be merciful to me, a sinner.' He'll help you to forgive your wife, and He'll cleanse you from the hatred and bitterness in your heart. Won't you do this now?"

He was very quiet, and I silently prayed for him. I know he was praying. There was a different expression on his face as he turned toward me. "God has helped you to forgive her, hasn't He? And God's forgiven you." He nodded his head, "With God's help I'm trying and I will," he replied.

Then I told him more about Christ, with emphasis on our Lord's love for us and forgiveness of our sins. When we parted, Mr. Smith put out his hand, and said, "Miss Rinker, you've helped save an old man from suicide. I haven't eaten or slept for three days. I didn't know what to do with myself. I've only had one thought — to kill myself. Now I've found Jesus. Thank you very much."

In my heart, I said, "Thank You, God."

A Train Ride

I'd had a strenuous week and felt exhausted as I boarded an evening train enroute to Butte, Montana. Thankful to be alone, I headed directly for the diner.

Scanning the menu, I paused to pray, "Lord, please don't let anyone sit across from me. I'm too tired to talk."

Glancing up I noticed the steward leading an attractive dark-haired woman toward me. Just as he pulled out the chair at my table, she recognized friends at the farther end of the car, so she thanked him, and joined them. Believing my prayer had been answered, I ordered my dinner with a sense of relief.

I had barely started eating when the same woman returned and sat down across from me. I murmured a polite, "Good evening." When the waiter had taken her order, she picked

up the white card placed on each table which contained Catholic, Protestant and Hebrew prayers for mealtimes. I'd already
examined it.

Aloud she said, "They all look the same to me."

"Yes," I replied, "they are all the same, except for one thing."
Inserting this bit of intrigue, I went on with my dinner.

The woman looked at me, then at the card. After reading it,
she said, "What do you mean? I don't see anything different
about them."

Looking directly at her, I answered, "The name of Jesus Christ
is in one of them." Then, resuming my dinner, I awaited her
response.

She re-examined the card. "How did you happen to notice?"

"Because that Name is very important to me," I replied.

Now she looked at me intently. Neither of us spoke. I prayed
silently and waited for God's guidance.

"Just what do you mean? In what way is it important? Who
are you?" She continued to ask many questions. Then she
told me about herself; married to an attorney, she and her
husband were church-members. Her sister was married to a
minister, and she had asked him many questions, but had never
been satisfied with his answers.

It was near midnight when our long talk and prayer together
ended. In parting she said, "You know, it was your reticence
to talk which prompted me to question you. I knew you knew
— and I had to know, too."

As I prepared for bed, I suddenly realized I was no longer
tired!

How can you speak to strangers?

Very simply — just as you'd want them to speak to you. Start
with the obvious and be alert for an opportunity to insert a bit
of intrigue which will provoke interest. Remember, that while
you do not "push" for a decision, it is important to give solid
information, so there will be an adequate foundation upon which
faith can be built. Remember, too, that faith is *in Someone,*
not something. "Believe on the Lord Jesus Christ and you shall
be saved."

I'm reminded of a salesman who sat behind me on a bus.

(*The point of contact*) I was putting on lipstick when I saw him in the little mirror I held and smiled.

"Can you see me?" he asked, then added, "Are you getting off at the next stop?" Answering his own question, he said, "You must be, since you're putting on fresh lipstick."

He was so friendly, I told him where I was going and that I'd be on the bus another two hours. I also decided on an adventure in conversation. I correctly guessed his occupation, and his age as 27. Impressed, he asked, "What kind of work do you do — fortune telling?"

(*The place for intrigue*) I laughed and said, "No, I counsel students."

"Well then, how about counseling me? I'm a crazy-mixed-up kid," and he grinned.

"I don't think you'd like my kind of counseling." Quietly I prayed for guidance.

"Yes, I think I would. Try me, please, try me."

"I can counsel you in two words, but I still think you may not like it."

He protested and continued to insist.

(*The beginning of a witness*) "The two words with which I'd begin to counsel you are *Jesus Christ.*"

His reaction was complete silence, followed by, "Okay, what's next?"

So that we might talk easier, I invited him to sit beside me. The next two hours we spent in deep discussion about Jesus Christ. What our Lord was like, what He said to those who were distressed or diseased, His attitude toward hypocrites, what He said concerning life and concerning death, His expression of love when He referred to Himself as the Shepherd and to us as His sheep, and most important of all, how and why He gave His life for us.

(*The follow-up*) "Faith," I explained, "comes from hearing with an open mind and heart, the message which comes directly from Christ." I asked how well he really knew the New Testament. When he admitted never having read it, I suggested a couple of recent translations readily available which I thought he would enjoy.

As we said good-by, I knew God went with him and would

continue to draw his heart to faith and trust in our beloved Saviour.

For your practical help:
1. Find the four steps in the last illustration.
2. Find these steps in the first two illustrations.

CHAPTER 14

Bringing Your Friends

"I am the Way, the Truth, and the Life," said Jesus, "no man comes to the Father except through Me." And how can we know about Him, unless someone tells us?

The most effective witness is that natural witness of friends who have found the Way themselves. Friends who talk calmly, sincerely, and even casually of Christ, and the difference He makes in their lives.

The question is, how can we do this?

I have two suggestions to share with you. One is the group approach — you invite your friend to go with you — we'll take this up in another chapter. The other is the personal approach — you talk with your friend face-to-face.

The Person-to-Person Approach

The plain truth is, many Christians are like the business man Paul Little writes about in his booklet, *Lost Audience* (IVCF). This man's increased church activity failed to compensate for the uneasy feeling he had about witnessing to his next door neighbors. Though very successful in business, he was at a complete loss when it came to sharing his faith with his neighbors. So he took the easy path — *isolation,* and avoided the problems!

Pehaps his Christian experience was something he referred to in general terms, or in theological terms, so he didn't know how to make a bridge. How *do* you talk about God in everyday terms? Or, perhaps he had never been exposed to a group who share specific ways in which Christ is Lord, and the difference it makes in their daily work and personal relationships.

Many people resent (and rightly so) the one-shot-testimony that zealous Christians sometimes force upon them. The non-

70

Christian, so cornered that he *must* listen, will see that it never happens again, if he has anything to say about it.

In bringing our friends to know Christ, we must be relaxed and natural. We must know how to take advantage of the subject matter at hand, and how to say just enough so that the door will be open for another conversation. We must be aware of God's timing. This always means wisdom, loving concern and sensitivity. Sometimes we must wait until some emergency, such as illness or death, comes to the family. Always we must be alert, caring, and listening to all our friend has to say.

"Last week I went over to my neighbor's with everything I was going to say firmly fixed in my mind. And what do you think happened?" a lady said to me the other day.

I guessed on the first try. "You forgot everything."

"How could you know?" was her astonished reply.

How did I know? She went with the old idea of "*giving* a *testimony*," not of listening (for the need). When we deliver unwanted goods, there's a convenient wastebasket as soon as our backs are turned. Do you know how to listen? Do you know how to ask a question, and then listen? I had to learn. I'm still learning, because it seems I have so much I want to say! But I don't want to "dump a delivery," I want a give-and-take conversation, where I can find out what my friend is thinking. Then I can make an intelligent contribution.

If you've been doing too much talking and not enough listening, you'll have to discover this before you can change. My friend Kay S. had such an experience. She had been visiting two Jewish friends who were hospitalized. After several weeks, she thought she ought to press for an opinion, as she'd told them many things about Jesus Christ.

"What do you think is *the* important thing out of all that I've told you?" she asked them eagerly one day, secretly hoping that they'd be ready to acknowledge Jesus as their Messiah.

Their answer floored her. "Well . . . we know how very much you want us to agree with all you say . . ."

"Oh," she said to me, "what did I do that was wrong?"

Listening is an art which can be cultivated.

Asking questions is also an art.

Making provocative statements is another art. Griping is a common human ailment. When you hear someone griping about money, or the weather, or his job, what do you think? What do you say? Here's an opportunity for you to make a statement which is really a question thrown out with hope and courage:

"You talk like God's dead!"

Back of this statement are many things that you've learned, that you know are important, that you want your friend to think about. God is alive. He does care. His love and His Presence make the difference. Griping only makes the problem greater. Everything is changed when you pray, "Thank You, Lord, that You're with me, so it really doesn't matter."

After you've made a statement like the one above, your friend's reaction will help you know where to go next in the conversation.

I can hear someone asking with incredulity, "Should you tell a non-Christian to give thanks?"

Why not? I know people who've actually been converted while they were giving thanks for the first time in their lives! The point is, *to whom* are you speaking? This makes the difference.

Remember to try a bit of intrigue, provoke his interest, but say enough to give him something to think about. Griping about anything indicates dissatisfaction, and when this goes into the area of one's work or personal relationships, that means deep need. Be alert and care enough to share what you know, because you do know what God is like. He is like Jesus Christ. Giving thanks for all things, lifts the dark anxiety and brings living trust in the ever-present, ever-loving Christ.

Two years ago, through my books, I started corresponding with six men in Indiana State Prison. Johnny was shy and ill at ease the first time we met him, but a few months later, he was open and ready to talk. I taught him the secret of "giving thanks," and I want to quote from a few of his letters:

"We were talking about thanking God. I'm learning to thank Him for all the little things that happen during the day. For every little thing. I find so many things to thank God for every day. I thank Him for your friendship and letters, because now I know right from wrong. I want to try when I get out to make all of my wrongs right, and God will help me. My whole life is changed because of Jesus. One thing I give thanks for is the answer to my prayers. You know I've been praying for my children. They called me to the visiting room the other day, and who walked in but my children! Maybe you think that wasn't a surprise. I was so happy I cried. That was the first time I had seen them in five years. God knows I prayed hard enough for that visit. That's why I give thanks, because God has already answered a lot of my prayers."

Earlier we stated that death or illness could be the open door of need which would give you the awaited opportunity. One of George's office-partners had an emergency operation. George was right there that night, with concern and with "special" reading material to nurture faith. He didn't stay long, that first visit, but his next visit was timed for his friend's recovery, and that day they had their first talk about faith and God.

After the loss of his wife, another business man said to his friend, a convinced Christian, "You know, my wife's death has left me a lonely man . . . tell me what do you believe about death?" His friend knew Jesus' teaching on death and the resurrection from John chapters 6 and 11; this moment he had prayed and waited for. It was worth waiting for.

This incident took place in a nurses' dormitory.

"Have you heard? Jean's fiancé was killed in an automobile accident!" The girls tip-toed and whispered as they passed Jean's door. Jean was packing her suitcase to attend the funeral. Mary Gordon found God's love in her identified with Jean, and she was unable to walk past that closed door. She knocked.

"All I could say to her," Mary told me afterwards, "was that I understood, because I'd lost my father not long before. I also said, 'I know there isn't too much I can do to help, but I know One who can. Try praying to Him. That helped me when I thought I couldn't stand it.'"

When Jean came back from that funeral, she looked for Mary at once. "You were the only girl in the whole dorm that came to my room after I got the telegram. I want to know you better. You were kind to me. I did pray, and it helped."

As a result of this friendship, Mary shared her personal faith and Jean gave her heart to Christ and became His follower. Strange as it may seem, there are some Christians who are so completely absorbed in their church activities, that they don't have any non-Christian friends. Do you? Are you willing to be involved for love's sake? Some friends of mine found a way.

Paul and Margaret Fromer (Editor, *His* magazine, IVCF) moved from Los Angeles to Downer's Grove, Illinois. Because they were total strangers in the community and wanted to meet people, they enrolled in a bi-weekly reading and discussion class called *Great Books*. During the first year's class, they listened to people, especially in the area of morals and religion. Gay F., mother of four children, seemed to speak freely on both subjects, so Margaret invited her to a Bible study in their home.

The first time she came, she asked the sixty-four dollar question: Will the heathen be lost? The second time she came, Paul asked her the question: "Are you a believer in Christ, or are you on the way?" She said she wasn't sure about the way, but she did believe in Christ. Paul told her she couldn't "cook up" faith, but as long as she believed in Christ, she could *trust in Him as her own personal Saviour.*

A few weeks later, Margaret brought Gay to a women's retreat. When we went around the circle, telling our names, why we came and who we really were, Gay volunteered, "Well, I'm only two weeks old! I guess I'm the newest Christian here." After that the story came out.

Is it true, that because of your knowledge of Christ, you are willing to be personally involved for love's sake?

Bringing My Friends to Christ

I remember the day Sue C. found Christ as her Saviour. (Or was it the day Christ found His little lost lamb who had strayed away?)

I was looking for her room-mate, but stopped to talk to Sue. Soon she was asking my help in preparing a Bible study for a group of students that met weekly. After a few moments, I sensed the subject she was preparing was really beyond her understanding and experience. Then I knew it was God's time for me to talk to her about her own relationship with Jesus Christ.

Had she ever studied the first chapter of John? No, she hadn't. We turned to it, and read it aloud together. I suggested we use the first 14 verses for the weekly study, and she agreed.

Reading the twelfth verse, I asked, "Sue, have you ever opened your heart to receive Jesus Christ? Have you ever invited Him into your life?"

Her answer was straight to the point. "No, I never have, but I'd like to."

The twelfth verse reads, *"But to those who did receive Him, He granted ability to become God's children, that is, to those who believe in His name."* There were two things for her to do, and then one thing that God would do for her.

She found them: receive Him and believe in His name. Did she believe in His name? Yes, but what was His name? Isn't His name Jesus?

We started at verse 1. *"In the beginning was the Word, and the Word was with God, and the Word was God."* Who was the Word? We tied verse 1 with verse 14, "And the Word became flesh and tented (lived) among us." Jesus is the Word, God's word to us. Then we read verse 1 again, and put Jesus' name into each place that said, *Word.*

"In the beginning was Jesus, and Jesus was with God, and Jesus was God." Jesus was the Word of God made human, made flesh. God has spoken to us through and in Jesus. Jesus is the living Word.

"Yes, I believe in Him. I believe in His name."

Carefully we went through those 14 verses, and found five names for Him: The Word, God, Life, Light of men, and True Light. She believed them all, and we talked about Him some more. Yes, she was ready to receive Him into her heart. Yes, she believed He died for her sins.

There was only one thing left to do. We did it together. We gave thanks. Sue's thankfulness brought tears, so simply and sincerely was it given.

For a little follow-up, for her to continue thinking, I asked her to finish reading that first chapter of John, and see how many more names of Jesus she could find.

Sue became a spontaneous witness for Christ among her friends, and several of them came to know Him through her witness.

Then there was Ken O., a friend of Jack's. I've known Jack since before we were teenagers in North Dakota! Ken was a bit shy of me, because I'd been a missionary, but soon he felt at ease. After we'd met a few times, he was my friend, too. I didn't try to bring up the subject of religion or God, I wanted to be his friend and let him know I was just another person like himself.

One night he came to hear me speak on *Prayer*, and the heart-intimacy possible between God and man which sets one free. As I spoke, I saw his wide-open heart through his eyes, and I said to myself, "Why, he's becoming a believer right there in his seat!" (Ever since I heard Jim Rayburn of Young Life Campaign speak on the subject, I have always had faith, and tried to speak from the platform in such a way that anyone listening could become a believer right in his seat. "According to your faith, be it unto you," Jesus said. It's true.)

After the meeting closed, as I shook hands with him, I said, "Ken, you believe in this Jesus, don't you?"

He looked at me as though to say, how do you know? and audibly replied, "Yes, I do."

I suggested we make our way to the back of the room, so we could talk quietly for a moment. When we got there, I asked Ken if he'd ever put his trust in the Saviour before, and he said, "No."

We simply stood there with bowed heads and *gave thanks*. What else was there to do? He believed. His giving thanks was the seal of the transaction between himself and God. Since then he has grown in the knowledge of both the written and the living Word of God.

As I drove home that night, I thought, *How really simple it is to reach people who have not been "conditioned" by wrong approaches.* And then with startling clearness another thought etched itself indelibly on my mind, "There must be hundreds of people just like Ken, who only need to know how much God loves them in order to put their trust in Jesus Christ."

For you to think about:
1. How do you talk about God in everyday terms?
2. Have you taken the initiative, for that certain friend, to see if there is any response . . . or interest? The secret is, broach the subject and find out.
3. How would you answer a person who asked, "Should I be witnessing to my neighbors? What should I say?"

4. Read carefully Jesus' words found in Mark 11:22-24 and John 16:24. Do you know how to pray a "faith-sized" request? It is a request for a particular situation, in which you pray for a special person or thing, and ask only for that which you can really believe God will do, for that particular time. Then you climb a step at a time — like going upstairs — waiting, believing, giving thanks, obeying, until the goal (the answer) is reached. (Read Chapter 10 in *Prayer — Conversing With God.*)

CHAPTER 15

Questions People Have Asked

The questions used in this chapter were asked in writing by young people in training for some special phase of Christian service. I chose these out of more than 100 questions gathered from recent conferences and workshops. The original wording has been retained, and even this should speak volumes to those of you who are learning new lessons on witnessing.

1. *How long should you know a friend before you talk to him about Christ?*

   Listen for inner guidance in your heart. Be natural. Be yourself. Watch for the guide-posts: your friend's interests, his needs, and things which disturb him. Sooner or later the subject of what you believe and why is bound to come up.

2. *What is the best way to introduce Jesus Christ into a conversation with someone who doesn't know Him?*

   It is easy to talk about Someone you love and trust. Don't try to get the person converted; instead share with him your knowledge and experience with Jesus. Let God do the rest. Trust Him. (Have you read chapters 9, 10 and 13?)

3. *I can't seem to get started. I can't get to the place where I'm able to say to someone, "What do you think (know/believe) of Jesus Christ?"*

   Since religion and politics are frequent topics of discussion, you can start with a casual question: What is your concept of God? Or, I don't think we've ever discussed religion, are you interested? Or, try the questions suggested in chapter 10. Keep alert and sensitive. You will know when to turn the conversation to Jesus Christ.

4. *I've known a friend for a few months, and have never told him I'm a Christian. How do I go about letting him know?*

> The answers to the first three questions should help you. My book, *The Years That Count* (pp 106-109) contains a story which answers your question. Pray for courage, faith and strength and you will receive them. Your conduct and unconscious influence will already have told him that you do have a faith to live by. You are now ready for a verbal witness. You might try, "There's something I've been wanting to tell you for a long time." He'll ask what it is, and in all probability you'll be surprised by his openness. You already know God *does* answer prayer. Apply this truth.

5. *How do you meet the opposition of a Roman Catholic friend?*

> In what way has he opposed you? On what subject? Why not agree on the central object of your faith, Jesus Christ. Love him and be his friend. Don't try to convert him to your ideas. Remember God loves him more than you do. You might ask him, "How personal is your faith?" Or, you might lend him a modern translation of the New Testament, so that he can see that it is understandable. (See notes at close of Chapter 9.)

6. *If a person gets angry whenever you mention your Christian life, should you quit saying anything in order to remain friends?*

> Yes, quit saying anything and be friends. Love him for himself. But listen to him. Seek clues to determine whether he is bluffing or really wants to know about God. Have you mentioned, at the right time, the importance of God's love for him? Or, that God cares for him? Your friend is not interested in "your Christian life." Like most people, he is interested in himself. There's a difference in knowing about God and knowing about the Christian life. The first is objective, the second subjective. Your problem may be that both your timing and your subject matter are inopportune. Study him, pray for him, love him and wait. Jesus Christ will one day enter your conversation. Since you seem to have started off on the wrong foot, this may

take time. Ask God to grant you patience and to guide you.

7. *What if a person gets you side-tracked to doctrinal arguments which are not pertinent to his own salvation?*
   a. He may need some knowledge on these subjects before faith can operate. Argument never won anyone. Avoid it.
   b. If the person is a mature adult and capable of discussion (not argument, there's a difference) you will find discussion with him profitable. You can both learn. Remain alert for the proper time to ask, What do you think/believe about Jesus Christ?
   c. If the person is young or immature, I'd simply say, casually and quietly, "I don't really think that ———— (name the subject) is the most important thing. What's important is, your belief concerning Jesus Christ."

8. *How do you witness to a friend who is a good church member but who doesn't know the Lord?*

   In the ways already discussed, but first it is wise not to assume he doesn't know the Lord. Have you ever heard of "unborn believers"? A good discussion about Jesus, His claims, His promises, and who He is, will guide you both into positive channels. The new life, or new birth, is a *result* of believing in Jesus. Avoid the danger of giving your friend spiritual indigestion by trying to push him into the *results* of faith before he knows the *Person* of his faith. It is well to remember the wisdom of trusting people to God. It works. Try it. (P.S. Have you shared any religious literature with him? A good magazine of Christian experience is *Faith at Work*, 8 West 40th St., New York 18, N. Y., or *His* Magazine, 1519 N. Astor, Chicago 10, Ill.)

9. *I have a girl friend who is not a Christian. She refuses to accept the fact that there is a God. What can I do to help her?*

   Have you shown her that you love her, even if she can't agree with you?
   Ask if her intellectual knowledge of Jesus Christ has

kept pace with her collegiate thinking? Suggest she would probably enjoy J. B. Phillips' translation, *The New Testament in Modern English.*

Ask a few quiet questions. Even if she appears unresponsive and resistive, she will remember your questions and her mind may come up with the answer later. Questions such as: Have you ever considered the claim made by Jesus Christ? Do you know what He said about Himself?

If you are strongly convinced Jesus came to show us what God is like, you will have no difficulty making your friend aware of your conviction. Just don't force any issue. Remember Jesus never "pushed."

10. *A non-Christian I know, cannot see the value of appealing to anything but his own reason. He feels that the only way to prove there is a God, and the need for salvation, is to prove it by rational thinking. How can one begin to show this person that there is an authority outside his own reason?*

After you ask him what he thinks about Jesus Christ, follow his answer with, "Are these your own ideas? Have you really read what He said about Himself?" Leave him with the subject open. Try intrigue and curiosity. Don't try to tell him everything you know. Let him find out some things for himself, which he will when he is ready. God will be with him when you aren't.

11. *How do you deal with someone who will not accept the Bible and relegates a Christian's experience to a psychological response?*

I'd say "someone" has the wrong subject for a frontal attack! Find out what he thinks about Jesus Christ. He will not accept the Bible nor the validity of a Christian experience until his thinking has changed regarding Christ.

Ask, if with an unprejudiced mind, he has read what Jesus said about Himself? Have you loaned him a modern translation? If not, why not do so? Tell him you would enjoy hearing what he thinks of it, and believe he will find it intellectually challenging, and quite different from what he has read in the past. And indeed, it

will be different! He will be discovering Jesus Christ!
Trust God's Spirit to work in your friend's heart. God
will nurture the seeds of thought you have planted.

12. *What is a story or illustration to give to the self-righteous
person?*

One who is self-righteous is egotistically self-centered,
not Christ-centered. Such a person is often irritating
to others including Christians! This person needs your
patience, love and understanding. Above all, keep
yourself in check. Be courteously objective in what you
say. Avoid any involvement concerning doctrine or
dogma. Strive to help him get a "new look" at the
Saviour.

Have you shared with him the way Christ's love has
changed you? Your outlook? How Christ enters every
aspect of your life, your plans?

13. *How do you explain the word "saved" other than by using
scripture? How can we get out of the habit of using language which we've grown up with, but which is meaning-
less to them? Words like, born-again, washed in the blood,
salvation, etc.?*

These words do have meaning for Christians. In help-
ing others to understand their meaning why not start
with Jesus Christ? It is *belief in Him* which matters.
Be sincere and let your love show. Don't be in a hurry.

14. *How do you end a conversation with a person who is not
ready to accept Jesus, but you want to leave him as a friend
and with a challenge?*

Have you read the stories in chapter 13, especially the
last one? And have you read the above answers? Simply leave him thinking about Jesus Christ and wanting
to find out more about Him, but wanting to go directly
to the source book, the Bible.

15. *How far should you go at the place you work with a personal testimony? Is my life enough to influence them for
the Lord?*

Quoting from the first page of chapter 9: "The spoken
word is never really effective unless it is backed up by
the life. The living deed is inadequate without the

spoken word. The reason for this is obvious. No life
is good enough to speak by itself. Any person who says,
'I don't need to witness; I just let my life speak,' is
unbearably self-righteous." When you have won a
hearing, by your life, by your friendship, then you can
speak. I feel certain your spoken testimony should
not be to a crowd, but to a single person.

16. *When someone at work asks you about your faith, how
should you approach the subject? Come right out and
say, "You're a sinner and need a Saviour," or soften it up
a bit?*

Come! Come! You know human nature well enough
to know such a subjective approach produces resistance!
You also know God's love will help you start properly.
Have you asked Him to help? If not, your first step is
to do so.

Why not invite that person to have lunch with you?
Indicate your respect for his judgment and that you
would like to tell him about your experience. Suggest
you prefer to discuss it with him when you can both
relax and have more time.

"And I, if I be lifted up from the earth,
    will draw all men unto me" (John 12:32).

CHAPTER 16

Belonging to a Group

It was with mixed feelings that I attended my first Faith at Work fellowship group many years ago.

"My chief problem," a young man was speaking, "is that I'm late everywhere I go. I keep people waiting, and inconvenience everyone. I know this is wrong. Yeah, I do have an alarm clock, but I don't get up when it rings. I guess I need your prayers for getting-up courage every time that bell rings!"

I listened with amazement. So tardiness could be a fault one could pray about! Where had I been? mentally I asked myself. Now I've made it a life-habit to bring everyday situations to the Lord in prayer or prayer-thoughts.

That group, and many others like it, have since been "used" in my life as I've seen my brother honestly face his shortcomings and do something about it. Recognizing that most human failure is due to pure selfishness or laziness, it does help to say things aloud and be willing for others to pray.

Listen to these people for a moment. They are members of a little fellowship group:

"I'm out of a job, but I've asked God to lead me to the right place, and I know He will."

"You all know I've just come from the hospital and I've been praying for a job, and I've got one! Thank God."

"I finally got things out in the open, and I've surrendered my whole life to the Lord."

"After so much struggling, at last I see that my main trouble is getting my eyes on other people; thinking that this one or that one is my ideal. I've finally seen that my eyes must be on Jesus Christ, and not on people."

"I need your prayers. I confess to impatience and irritation with my 12-year-old son, just because he is beginning to have a mind of his own."

84

A fellowship group like this is composed of men and women or it may be a men's group, or a women's group. They get to deeper levels and honest interchange of experiences or desires in their sharing and their praying. Then comes a period of growth, and finally of reaching out to help others, and inviting them to the group.

Irving Harris, editor of *Faith at Work* Magazine, writes: "Fellowship groups are for people who accept the Christian faith as an unfolding way of life — changing, deepening, developing. And for those who want to discover spiritual reality, but who are still groping. And for all who are ready to apply personal religious experience to their wider social, business, or political activities. Far more likely in a group than in public worship, an enquirer will find a handle to take hold of — a backslider a place to begin again.

"The central purpose of fellowship is to discover more skill in passing faith on to others — how to witness in words as well as by example. How to relate discoveries in private life to the home and to the job. To see, to pray, to grow, to share and to apply — these are the verbs at the heart of the Christian cells.

"Even the group in which conversions take place, and where individuals find it possible to become vocal about what God has done for them — even such a fellowship falls short of the mark unless it forms an organic part of the Body of Christ, the Church. Groups *per se* are not an answer, nor an end in themselves. God's love and life, as mediated in Jesus Christ, are the heart's deepest desire, and the need of the Church and the world."

If it is true that you feel "witnessing" is impossible for you, have you tried a fellowship group? Here you will find others like yourself, and together you can gain strength by facing weakness. Your brother's weakness will become your strength.

There's a time for living what you believe. There's a time for speaking about what you believe. There's a time for asking your friend what he believes. And there's a time to invite your friend to the fellowship group with you.

Ten years ago my personal testimony was written up and published in an issue of *Faith at Work*. Since then I've taken the magazine, helped in week-end conferences the past few years, and am presently writing a column for the magazine. This sharing body of men and women from churches of various denominations works within their respective churches. Conferences of witnessing lay people are sponsored in lieu of the usual evangelistic meeting. During the week-end after each session, talk-it-over groups meet immediately so everyone is exposed and has an opportunity to express himself. "Christianity is not taught — it is caught!"

What happens when a church invites lay people for a *Faith at Work* conference?

A recent week-end meeting in an Anglican Church in St. Thomas, Ontario, Canada, has already seen the following results: a dozen or more folk are now meeting regularly in small groups; a woman physician has already gone to a nearby church to tell of her new experience in Christ; and a Bible study group has been re-vitalized.

FAW sponsored such a conference in the United Presbyterian Tabernacle of Youngstown, Ohio. This fall when I visited Robert and Mary Mulholland, I was impressed with what God was doing in their midst.

"We had a funeral service and buried our mid-week meeting," Bob told me.

"What happened then?" I was interested.

You should hear them tell it. For a number of weeks the pastor taught a class of married couples. They then spread out in *fellowship groups,* each couple starting a mid-week meeting in their own home. Instead of one small group of 15 people meeting once a week, there are now more than 8 groups with some 80 participating! Best of all, friends and neighbors regardless of church affiliation feel free to come into homes for relaxed study, discussion and prayer.

My question to Bob: "Do these fellowship groups provide for an easier witnessing situation, at the time, or afterwards?"

His answer: "*Much* easier witnessing situation, both at the time and afterwards. Great openness during the meetings. People who never thought they could or would witness are sharing their faith in Christ. Those attending often call one another afterwards. They tell their friends what's happening."

Question: "Are you as enthusiastic now, as before?"

Answer: "More so than ever. This is the answer for *today's* church. We don't limit the Holy Spirit to one avenue, nor do we limit the next generation if God should lead them differently."

Question: "What would you say are the most encouraging aspects of this group-fellowship?"

Answer: 1. "We keep our meetings open and free. No set program, though all use Scripture for a basis for discussion. There is much freedom to talk.

2. "We use conversational prayer exclusively in most meetings. Result, people who thought they could never pray — having been used to listening to orators — now joyfully pour out their hearts to the Lord.

3. "Faith has grown in all. People are now *expecting* answers to prayer and getting them! Souls have been *saved*, sick have been *healed*, needs have been met, and lives have been changed. There's a constant stream of witnessing to 'what happened last week.'

4. "There is far more *love* in evidence than ever before. Great heart openness to all. One group had a neighboring woman attend after she had fortified herself with three beers. That night she accepted the Lord and is now a member of the Church.

5. "We have to watch the danger of becoming ingrown. We keep things 'shook up' by getting groups to meet together from time to time. We encourage visiting from one group to another. And we get as many people as possible to go to every FAW conference within driving distance. We've gone to Harrisburg, Greensburg, Pittsburgh in Pennsylvania and Warren, Sharon, and North Lima in Ohio. The group members give out as well as take in. Result: new stimulus."

Rev. Mulholland closed his letter by asking, "Do you wonder that we are tremendously enthusiastic about our prayer fellowship groups which have been going on now for two years?"

There apparently are some churches who will try everything except submit themselves either to person-to-person witnessing or to the honesty of real group fellowship.

Joseph Bayly's *The Gospel Blimp* (Windward Press) carries the subject of *how-to-witness-without-being-personal* to the last ludicrous extremity! The Christians of a certain local church thought they had tried everything, but nothing seemed to produce results. Finally they came up with a novel idea sure to work! Sure to attract the non-Christians! They would broadcast the Gospel on TV and radio, from a Gospel Blimp! They opened an office, hired a dozen men, set up business, spent thousands of dollars, and congratulated themselves that they were "spreading the Gospel"!

They succeeded in alienating the whole community when *their program* "cut out" other desired programs. One of their original committee finally saw the folly of their frenzied spending and activity, resigned, and began to witness to his neighbor (after first apologizing for the disturbance the Gospel Blimp was causing)! You should read it for yourself. It has a message for all who want to witness to Jesus Christ.

In contrast to the above "scheme" by people with a good motive, read the following story. Here are the brave, bold words of a man who knew God had spoken to him regarding the importance of lay people witnessing to personal encounter with God.

St. Stephen's (Episcopal) Church in Houston, Texas, is having an unusual group experience in the area of witnessing, following an insight into the meaning of I Corinthians 14. Six years ago, the rector, Claxton Monro, was convinced that God had given him this vision: "The Witnessing Fellowship of Christian Laymen is destined to become, in the decades ahead, the center of authority and power in the Church; and God is going to speak through this witnessing community as He spoke through the Bible at the time of the Protestant Reformation."

How does this work out in actual practice?

"Since 1954 every Sunday at St. Stephen's a layman has given, in an evening service, a witness about the action of Jesus Christ in his life. In the same service the Rector also speaks briefly on one of eight basic Christian Disciplines.* This is followed by small group meetings for men and for women, where laymen tell how the keeping of Christian discipline has helped their life of faith. Afterwards there is coffee for all, a book table, and informal conversation which results in person-to-person encounter, and more witnessing.

"Since 1958 there have been a growing number of weekly groups for the growth of believers. They meet mostly in homes and not on Sundays. Here the Bible and what it is saying to each group member is the focal point of interest. Here are said together the Seven Disciplines for Church Members, and here each has an opportunity to pray from his heart. This

*See footnotes at end of chapter for a list of the Eight Disciplines.

Faith, Study and Prayer Fellowship is making its vital contribution to the growth of believers. In most of these groups men meet with men, and women with women. There are some mixed groups, too. Probably more than 150 persons (about 15% of the church membership) now are active in these groups. Also attending these groups are men and women from other Episcopal parishes and other denominations. This is an expression of God's ecumenical movement on the grass root level.

"St. Stephen's has also had weekly evangelistic home meetings out of which have come many new converts who have developed into strong Christians. This has led to the conviction that such home meetings are indispensable to the evangelism of the Church. Attendance ranges from 12 to 40, and there is a special workshop to train lay leaders for these meetings.

"The purpose and spiritual structure of all this work is described in Ephesians 4:11-16."

Quoting from Claxton Monro's article from the September, 1961, issue of *Faith at Work:* "We believe that there is a new need for emphasis on basic spiritual disciplines which the individual can follow if he wishes to grow in his life in Christ.

"What men are seeking today is a way of life which will make it possible for them to live with God and be aware of His constant Presence in their lives. In an age when there is great doubt about the Divinity of Jesus Christ and the inspiration of the Holy Bible, we find that the revelation of the love of God through the lives and witnesses of Christians has an effectiveness which is sometimes astonishing. The spiritual climate of this age makes it necessary for this ministry to be raised up, and we believe that what we are really doing is restoring to the Church the kind of approach to the Gospel that the Bible indicates was made in Apostolic times.

"Our experience tells us that it is through the layman's witness in the corporate life of the Church that unbelievers will be converted, and it is through their witnessing, teaching, evangelizing and shepherding that they will come to a deeper understanding of the Lord Jesus Christ. This will make them strong, believing, serving, worshipping members of the Body of Christ."

For Further Study:

1. For more information regarding The Witnessing Fellowship of Laymen, write for booklet, *Creating Christian Cells*, 75c, which contains Claxton Monro's article, *The God Who Speaks*. Order from: Faith at Work, 8 West 40th St., New York 18, N. Y.

2. *Eight Disciplines for Church Members*

   Purpose: to glorify God
   to strengthen the Church
   to help the world
   to grow in my Christian life

   In the Name of Jesus Christ Our Lord,
   As an expression of my love for God,
   I will do my best to:

   (1) Seek God's plan through a daily time of listening prayer and Bible reading.

   (2) Worship weekly in the Church with emphasis on Holy Communion.

   (3) Participate regularly in a weekly faith, study and prayer fellowship.

   (4) Give regularly a definite grateful share of my income to the spread of God's Kingdom through the Church and in the world.

   And, as an expression of love for my neighbor, I will do my best to:

   (5) Pray daily for others with thanksgiving.

   (6) Exercise faithfully my particular ministry in the fellowship of the Church.

   (7) Speak and act so that my daily life is a witness to the love of God in Christ as I have come to know it.

   So help me God.

CHAPTER 17

Understanding the Cultist

The title of this chapter was chosen because I believe it holds a secret for those who find it difficult to talk understandingly with friends following a cult.

What is a cult? Walter Martin (*The Rise of the Cults*, Zondervan), defines it: "Cultism is any major deviation from orthodox Christianity relative to the cardinal doctrines of the Christian faith."

Most of the books I've read about cults were exposés of their doctrinal errors: their lack of belief in the Bible, in the Trinity, and in the deity of Jesus Christ. These books gave histories of various cults, and quoted warnings from the Bible regarding those who depart from sound doctrine. They also offered various methods for gathering information considered useful in refuting cultists.

However, I found very little in these books describing the kind of people favoring cultism. I do not personally know too many "cultists." Those I do know are alert, intelligent, sensitive, seeking people. Yet, more often than not, in their seeking they have found only blind dogma without a living experience, or rigid doctrine devoid of love.

I'd like to share with you a few of my experiences with people either in a cult, or who have recently left one. What they sought and what they failed to find.

Last year I was visiting my sister, Denise Adler in Seattle. She told me of a woman who was studying one of the cults. Yes, the woman had grown up in a certain church, but having no satisfactory solution for her problems, had turned to this particular cult. Her basic problem? Strained and hostile family relationships resulting from the unfair settlement of her father's will.

Her classes were designed to give her practical help in loving those who differed with her, and to instruct her in disciplining her own mind; to recognize and affirm the Truth when it appeared. It never occurred to her to question the "doctrinal beliefs" either of the material she read or the instruction she received. She desperately needed help and was receiving it. Her blood pressure returned to normal and she was now about to face the offending members of her family with dignity and love.

Yes, people do find some help and peace through such seeking, but they need help in finding Jesus Christ, who is Himself the source of peace.

Before writing this chapter, I placed a long distance call to my friend Carolyn B. I knew she had been an active Christian Scientist for 25 years. I had several questions to ask her.

Q: *How far did you go in Science?*

Ans: I started with class instruction. Several years later I served three years as First Reader in my church, followed by three years as Second Reader.

Q. *Did you then feel you had found the Truth?*

Ans: No. So many of their teachings about God are mental concepts. This always secretly disturbed me.

Q: *Do you now feel that you have found the Truth?*

Ans: Absolutely. I know that Jesus is the living Christ, for I walk with Him and talk with Him each day.

Q: *Why did you leave Christian Science?*

Ans: One day I asked a clerk in a religious store to recommend a book for me to read. It was a very personal story of one whose life had been transformed by the Lord Jesus. My own eyes were opened to the need of a personal Saviour. I'd always felt a certain incompleteness. I gave my heart and my life to Jesus Christ and became His child.

Q: *Based on your own experience, what word of advice would you give to those desiring to witness to their friends involved in some cult?*

Ans: Only one thing will attract — the living, radiant Jesus Christ as the center of their lives. Science only offers peace of mind through a philosophy of life. One is always making statements of Truth; relying on self for growth and strength. True strength and peace of mind come to us as the gift of Jesus when we permit Him to enter our lives and dwell in our hearts.

The first step toward understanding those following a cult is to realize *they are seekers after truth.* Should you question my use of the term, *Truth,* I suggest you re-examine the claims of Jesus. Especially the "I am's." I am the Good Shepherd. I am the Bread of Life. I am the Door. I am the Way, the Truth, and the Life. I suggest you also read the discourses containing these same truths. If the New Testament contains any one message above another, it is that Christ is the center of our faith, of our life, now and hereafter. There can be no compromise. No substitution for our Lord. Only when Christ enters your heart can a New Life begin. Only then is one literally born again! Such Truth was never meant to be self-contained. It is meant to be shared.

Regardless of who may knock at your door, hand you literature, or speak to you in public, be courteous. Remember that for many who approach you, Jesus is respected only as a good man and a great teacher. If Jesus Christ has been born into your heart, and you know Him, talk with Him, and experience His transforming touch — then you, too, have a message for others. The vital message of *Jesus Christ:* our living Lord, loving Saviour, and ever-present God! Keep your approach gentle. Let God's love be reflected when you ask another what they believe about Jesus Christ. Follow your inquiry with attentive courtesy, listening to their response. A positive witness given in love and kindness will be remembered long after your face is forgotten.

My last story concerns Beatrice. During my years as a staff member for Inter-Varsity Christian Fellowship, I made regular visits to a teachers' college in Oregon. One fall, during the opening week, the house mother said, "I'm sorry, Miss Rinker, but I don't have a room for you this time. Would you mind sharing with someone?" In this way I met Beatrice, who appeared to be ten years my senior.

As soon as we were alone, Beatrice said, "Well, I'm glad they put you here with me, and not with some teenager! We can have some good talks together."

"I'd like that," I replied, "but I'm only staying three days. I'm not a student."

"You're not!" was her incredulous and disappointed reply. "What are you?"

"I'm a counselor for a religious group on campus."

"Oh, well, I'm a searcher for Truth so we can still have some good talks."

I know there was a positive reaction in my voice as I followed her lead, "You are! How interesting! Where have you looked? Where have you searched?"

She delayed replying to my question to show me photographs of her grown daughter and son. As a widow, she had taught school to support them. At that time, the State of Oregon permitted teachers to hold a position under a certificate, if they continued their education during the summer. Every summer she had gone to school, and this was the term when she would complete her work toward her Bachelor's degree.

Returning to my original questions, she answered, "Where have I searched?" Then added, "Everywhere. I've searched everywhere for Truth, and I'll find it.'

"Tell me," I urged, "right from the beginning, just where did you start?"

"During my childhood I attended a certain Protestant Church, but," she continued, "by the time I reached high school I realized I had not yet found what I wanted. I decided to try another church but found it no different so enrolled in a class of instruction on Roman Catholicism."

When she paused, I asked, "Did you become a Catholic?"

"No," she smiled, "I didn't. I found their presentation of Truth far too dogmatic.'

"What then?" I asked.

"I attended the Christian Science Church and studied *Science and Health With Key to the Scriptures* which I found made sense, but did not entirely satisfy me, so I sought elsewhere."

"Where?"

"I tried to study Swedenborgianism but found it too philosophical and mystical. But I believe Truth can be found in this world and I believe I shall someday find it."

"Yes," I replied, as convinced as she was, "I believe you will." By this time I was sure our meeting was no accident. She did not yet know it, but she was about to make the greatest discovery of Truth in her life — *Jesus Christ*. God knew, and I knew. I waited and listened, fascinated by her tenacious search.

"The next thing I studied was Rosicrucianism, which is as you know, obscure and highly secret, and claims possession of wisdom that can only be imparted to the initiated. However, I lost interest, since even the various Rosicrucian societies are not in agreement as to whether Rosicrucianism is primarily philosophical or religious in the quest for Truth."

"Where did you look next?" I urged her on, with a genuine interest to see what she would discover.

"Well, I taught school in Utah about that time, and one night two young men knocked at my door." She paused.

We said it together, "The Mormons."

"Yes," she continued, "the Mormons. And for the next two years as they came weekly to teach me, I learned more about the Bible from them than I ever knew in my whole life."

"Are you a Mormon, then?"

She laughed again. "No, I'm not. You see, I couldn't take The Book of Mormon and the Golden Tablets which Joseph Smith was supposed to have found in a New York hill. But I did learn a lot from those boys. They really knew their Bibles."

There was a quiet moment. In my heart I was praying. A woman searching for the Truth! I had learned how to project His love (through prayer and my thoughts) to her. The room was full of His love, and yet so far I hadn't said anything. I was finding out where she had sought Truth.

"That was last year," Beatrice was saying, "that I studied the Bible with the Mormons."

"So, what about now?"

She pointed toward her desk. "See that book over there, it's on Zen-Buddhism. If Truth is there, I'll find it."

There was another moment of quiet reflection. Then she turned to me, "What about you? Where do you think one finds Truth?"

"I'll answer that question, by asking you one," I said, having waited for this moment. "*What do you think about Jesus Christ?*"

She did not answer immediately and appeared to be thinking. Finally she said, "I do not believe in Him." With this she began pacing about the room, and repeated, "No, I don't believe in Jesus Christ! Nor do I believe He's God. He can't be God. It just isn't logical! No, I simply don't believe He's God!"

Watching her, I quietly listened and waited without interrupting, noting the transition in her statements from "I don't believe" to "He can't be."

Suddenly she turned to me and asked, "How do you know He's God?"

"I didn't say He was. But now that you've asked me, let me assure you that *I do know* He is God, and so can you!"

I opened my New Testament, and handed it to her, asking her to read aloud.

"In the beginning was the Word, and the Word was with God, and the Word was God. He Himself was in the beginning with God. Through Him everything came into being and without Him nothing that exists came into being."

She paused, and with a never-to-be-forgotten expression looked up at me. "It says here, that He was God. I've read this before, but for some reason never realized the Truth of what it says."

Together we examined Hebrews 1, Colossians 1, Philippians 2, and John 14. We talked long and quietly, and then she asked, "Rosalind, will you teach me to pray?" Kneeling beside her bed, I taught Beatrice how to pray — slowly, sentence by sentence, as in the past I'd taught my Chinese friends. For her had come the end of seeking. She had at last found Truth — "I am the Way, the Truth and the Life . . . He who has looked on Me has looked on the Father" (John 14:6, 9).

The three days I spent with Beatrice were followed by two months of correspondence. The wonderful, happy letters she sent were a delight. Then came the news that she had died of a sudden, brief illness. Quietly, I thanked God that she had indeed completed her B.A. degree, only this time it was Born Again, not Bachelor of Arts!

For reading and meditation:

"I am the Resurrection and the Life; the believer in Me will live even when he dies, and everyone who lives and believes in Me, shall never, never die" (John 11:25, 26).

"You will know the truth and the truth will set you free" (John 8:32).

"And I, when I am lifted up from the earth, shall draw everyone to myself" (John 12:32).

"For this is My Father's will, that everyone who sees the Son and believes in Him, shall have eternal life, and I will raise him up at the last day" (John 6:40).

"I am the Bread of Life, so that anyone who eats of it may not die. I am the Living Bread . . . if anyone eats of this bread, he will live forever. Just as the life-giving Father sent Me and I live through the Father, so he who nourishes on Me shall live through Me" (John 6:48-51, 57).

CHAPTER 18

Reaching Your Family

Everywhere I go, people want to know, "How can I reach my family?" We can trust our loved ones to God. He loves them more than we do. But He does need our cooperation, and herein is love in action.

My dear mother went to be with Jesus in August, 1961. She would have been 85 the following week. She knew I was writing this book and sent me one of her favorite books on Reaching Your Family. The book is titled, *Household Salvation* (Sword of the Lord Publishers, Wheaton). I found only the first chapter was concerned with this subject, and that was why she valued the book. I guess I must have had it in my possession about a year, and she kept writing for me to send it back to her! Now she's gone — but she doesn't need a book anymore to encourage her to believe that all her six children and ten grandchildren will "make Heaven." She knows her prayers will be answered! She knows everything. She knows how they are being answered right now!

The greatest desire of Christian parents is to be able to stand before God some day and say, "Behold, I, and the children You have given me." Acts 16:31 is the verse my mother "stood on" for her family, *"Believe on the Lord Jesus Christ, and thou shalt be saved, and thy house."* That's the King James translation; the Berkeley Bible reads, "Believe on the Lord Jesus and you will be saved and your family, too."

The background story of this verse is found in the sixteenth chapter of Acts. The jailer was converted with his whole family and great joy filled their hearts. The jailer cried, "Men, what must I do to be saved?" Paul answered, "Believe on the Lord Jesus and you will be saved and your family, too."

Someone may say, "But my loved ones must believe for them-

98

selves, and they will if I pray for them." Yes, that's right,
each one must believe for himself. But the Bible gives every
parent the right to pray for, and believe for the salvation of
his children. And God answers prayer.

Some passages in the Bible encourage parents to pray for
their families: *Noah*, Hebrews 11:7; *The Passover*, Exodus 12;
Rahab, Joshua 6:25; *Joshua*, Joshua 24:15; *Cornelius*, Acts 10:
2, 24, 33, 44.

The jailer believed for himself, and then the members of
his household believed for themselves. Father, mother, believe
for yourself, and then by faith claim your children and pray
until you can give thanks and know God has heard and will
answer. Son, daughter, you may believe God will hear and
answer prayer for your loved ones! Grandmother, pray, and
rejoice, God will hear your prayers!

I clearly remember my mother telling me she used to think
her heart would break if all of her children did not "make
Heaven," and in her anxiety she would weep before the Lord.
One day He spoke to her heart, "My child, I have heard your
prayers. Offer praise now. Offer thanksgiving. Do not be anxious,
and do not ask again." From that time, she never ceased giving
thanks.

John, the Beloved, in Revelation 5:8, tells us that the prayers
of the Christians on earth are kept in golden bowls, like incense
before the throne of God. No prayer is lost, and God will, in
His own time, answer all prayer.

Your teenager needs to hear father pray. He needs to hear
mother pray for him and for herself. He needs to know that his
parents trust him to God. Parental love expressed in prayer is
the most effective way there is to convince your child he is
loved.

After hearing me speak on this subject, a woman in Seattle
said, "Now I know what's been missing in our home. I have
fresh faith to believe that this will be the answer to our problem: we've a ten-year old adopted daughter, and nothing we
say seems to convince her that we truly love and want her.
We're going to have family prayers in our home . . . conversational prayer."

Last year an attractive teenager, who thought her parents
did not love her, rang our door-bell. Was it true? Didn't they

love her? Of course they loved her — she was the only daughter they had. They adored her. What made her think she was not loved? With deep resentment, she said to them, "You've never told me so."

How can you tell a rebellious teenager she, or he, is loved? They've forgotten the many times you've told them while they were growing up; they seem to have forgotten all the things you've done (and are still doing) for them. They're away and winging, with a maturing body and an immature mind, but they'll come back. Parents who remember their own confused adolescent years, reach out with protecting love to shield their child, and are baffled by the rebellion they meet. Remember, your child is a person, as you were a person during those searching years. Did you tell your parents everything? Did they ever find out? And you lived through it, and benefited by it, didn't you? Give your child a chance; he's as smart as you are.

But . . . love him, and pray for him, and pray with him.

When the daughter flung out that cruel accusation, in the above situation, "You don't love me. You've never told me so," I turned to the father with a question.

"Do you have prayer in your home? With your family?"

Slowly he shook his head "No" and then added, "Well, we do say grace at table, but it's the same one all the time."

Dr. V. Raymond Edman, president of Wheaton College, when asked if he had it to do over again, what he would do differently with his children, answered: "I would take more time, deliberately to be with my children. We would have more time for reading and praying together, for picnics and trips. Reading and praying together make love and security real to young hearts."

Here is an eye-opening letter: "I am a self-righteous mother. I've known it for a long time, and I've tried to remedy the situation. I've confessed it to my children, also to my husband, but they won't believe it. As they were growing up, I was so proud and self-righteous, and always right. So many of my friends have done the same damage. Some of their children are without Christ and will have nothing to do with their mother's religion. Will these same children go lost, while the mother goes merrily in through the Pearly Gates? I know God is just and will remedy things somehow. How did He ever dare to put even one of these little ones into our possessive hands? Of course, I've trusted God to make good where I've failed, and He has. All of my seven children are married, and they are all saved."

Yes, she's right, God "will remedy things somehow," because He is a just and loving God, and He has given Himself to us in Christ. He will remedy things beyond our understanding, and in keeping with His eternal heart.

The mother who wrote this letter had the right spirit; she saw and admitted her failure to her family. There is nothing which will break down barriers as quickly as admission of fault on the part of the parents. Healing and understanding result when this is accompanied by love and prayer together. When mother needs and receives help, the children feel there is "help" for them, too. Love is the example which will release God's light into the dark places in others. Where there is loving intention to reach out, the power of God's spirit is at work healing the bruised and broken.

But why wait to pray with them until they are in their teens?

The Roman Catholic Church asks only for the first seven years of a child's life. Those first important years are often overlooked by parents. A mother in the state of Washington knew the importance of this truth.

Marion and Byron J. have a family of seven. He is a college professor and the children are as creative as their parents. What impressed me was the conversation carried on around the supper table. There was interest, security, sensitivity as the children were encouraged to participate in the current subject. One day I said to Marion, "How is it your children are so well-integrated and secure?" She smiled and told me that she would let me in on her secret.

One night after supper, she put me into a dark corner in the master bedroom. Soon six-year-old Billy came prancing in, and up on the bed he went. Mother came in and shut the door. She reached for the Bible story book, and knelt by the bedside, reading to him within the circle of warm light that shut them in together. After the story, she held out both hands, and took his chubby ones into hers, while his little "behind" reared and twisted, and his legs thrashed about. He didn't seem to be paying any attention at all. Her prayer was simple and full of tender love, and his little prayer followed quickly. After she took him to his own room, she came back.

"I've given every one of my children 15 minutes every night

until they are 10 years old," she explained. "Sometimes it has
seemed impossible, but I've always managed, even if I had to
be late somewhere. They grow up *so* fast, and I have *so* little
time with them. I want them to know God loves them, and
that we do, too."

"Oh," said a lady at a recent women's retreat, "I wish someone had told me that story before mine grew up!" Every day is
a new beginning. God will help you. Start where you are. Start
now.

Perhaps your first start is with your husband. A lady in a
southern state spoke to me after a meeting, "Oh, I've done *all*
the things I shouldn't do, and I've alienated my husband. I
can't even talk to him about religion any more." Her husband
was an attorney. After a moment, I said, "Could you try something like this: 'Tom, I'm desperate. I need you. I know I've
said all the wrong things, and you think I'm a religious fanatic,
but I really need you. I need your clear, plain thinking to help
me. I don't want to go on alone without you. Let's start over.'"
The relief on her face was so evident, I felt certain her admission of need to him would begin to alter the situation.

Love does alter the situation. "Love one another as I have
loved you," Jesus left His commandment to us. Love does not
condemn the other for not being "saved" as you are. Love does
not try to change the other. Love accepts. Remember how much
God loves your family and that His constant love is reaching
for them daily. He loves them more than you do. You can't
make them over, so why try? Love them the way they are.
You *can* trust your loved ones to God. You can *learn* to trust
your loved ones with God.

Kathleen C. found Christ during a summer conference. Her
first longing was that her husband share the joy of new-
found faith. "We were an old married couple!" she said, "and
how was he ever going to change any of his ways!" She found
a way. When she returned, she shared with him what had happened to her, and then without urging him to do the same,
she began to do the changing herself. Previously she had posi-
tively hated garden-work, but now she went willingly to weed,
to hoe and to be with him in the garden he loved. She used to
be bored with the games he liked, now she found herself wanting to play his games with him. Yes, she won her husband,

because she let him see the change in her, instead of trying to change him.

This happened in Eugenia Price's family. She and her mother lived the Christian life before her father and her brother, and kept praying. One day Joe hit a big trouble-spot in his life, and when he said, "What really happened to Genie?" his mother led him to Christ. Then one night, after Genie spoke in the church where she grew up, she gave an invitation. One person came. It was her own father.

There is another obstacle in sharing your Christian faith with your wife or your husband. That is, lack of communication. Some couples never had it in the first place, others lost it somewhere and never found it again. In some homes there is no conversation about anything except money and food! Each goes his own way, and they share living quarters. This lonely-island type of living exists in so-called Christian homes, for rather than get a divorce, they decide to make the best of it. The human heart longs for understanding, and lack of communication with a loved one is almost worse than death!

I know I seem to talk as though prayer were a panacea for all ills! But this I believe: *God answers prayer.* When people talk to God, they can say things which they are unable to say to one another. They are able to be honest, to admit need, to ask forgiveness, because God's love is great enough. Human love, at its best, is limited.

One couple, married 40 years, heard this suggestion. They were good church-members, taught Sunday school, were good citizens, had grace-at-table, as well as Bible reading and prayer daily. But they had never prayed from their hearts, using the personal pronoun "I" when they meant themselves; they had always used the editorial "we" which can be so impersonal. It was after the wife heard my talk on "Love one another and open the communication lines by conversational prayer," that she went home and suggested they try it. Later she admitted that for years they had had no communication between them, and this simple kind of praying had so opened their hearts to God and to each other, that it was like a second honeymoon!

Several couples have told me that the best time for them to pray together is at night, after the light is out! God seemed nearer and it seemed easier to be honest. Communication lines are open!

"How can I speak to someone," said a lady, "who apparently knows the way of salvation, and yet never gives evidence of having received Christ as Saviour?" I knew she was referring to her husband.

We must trust our loved ones to God, and go about our way, trying to help someone else's loved ones. It's always easier to talk to someone outside the family. In the family, it is one's life that tells the story. I don't know why there seem to be more women with unsaved husbands, than husbands with unsaved wives. Contact with business and political life may have something to do with it. Some of these people go to church and do seem to know all about Christ.

Sometimes men in business feel that they are called on to participate in things that may not be in harmony with the church, and this hinders them from making an open decision. There are churches which impose specific regulations upon their members, which might be better left to the individual, to give him a choice and an opportunity to foster true maturity. By insisting upon conformity from the start, the bird is frightened away. Stacey Woods' father used to say — Never try to pull the feathers out of a live chicken — wait until he's dead — there'll be no squawking then!

For some time I have been working and speaking on the theory that there are many "unsaved believers" in our churches. I have had opportunity to try this theory.

In a recent Indiana city, I was entertained in a home where the lady said, "Before my husband comes home, I want to tell you he's not a Christian. I've been praying for years. He'll go to church with me, but that's all."

I asked her if she knew *why* he wasn't a Christian, and she said he never would tell her.

I liked Charles immediately. He was a salesman, with lots of stories, friendly and open. That night from the platform where I was speaking, I could see him easily. He was half-way back, at the end of the pew, leaning out a bit. He took in everything and the interest on his face was significant to me. After the meeting, all who wished to participate in "conversational prayer" were invited to the basement, where a circle of chairs had been prepared. Charles came, and I watched him push his chair back — he was half-in and half-out of the circle! I smiled to myself. An unsaved believer, probably a secret believer.

Later, eating cold turkey at the kitchen table, I looked right at him. "Charles, you're not an unbeliever. You're a secret believer in your heart!" He blustered a while, but I called his bluff: He was more than interested during the meeting. He came willingly to a *prayer meeting* — half-in and half-out — but he was there!

I turned to his wife, "Grace, you don't need to pray for his salvation anymore, your prayers are answered. Start giving thanks. *He's in.*" We both looked at him, and he grinned a great big broad grin and shrugged his shoulders! We gave thanks then, the three of us. Since that time the two of them pray together at the kitchen table.

"Christianity is not taught — it's caught!"

God grant to each one of us the Christian humility we must have to win our loved ones.

For your prayer time:

Have you really put your loved one into God's hands?
Can you cease your efforts, now, and give thanks?
You can trust your loved one to God.

THE ZONDERVAN PAPERBACK SERIES
96 pages each, 69c

THE POWER OF POSITIVE PRAYING — John Bisagno   No. 9238s
THE REBELLIOUS PLANET — Lon Woodrum   No. 12292s
YOU CAN WITNESS WITH CONFIDENCE — Rosalind Rinker
    No. 10714s
APOSTLE TO THE ILLITERATES (Frank C. Laubach)—David Mason
    No. 10141s
THE GOSPEL BLIMP — Joe Bayly   No. 12288s
FREEDOM FROM THE SEVEN DEADLY SINS — Billy Graham
    No. 9716s

128 pages each, 79c

A BIT OF HONEY (After-dinner speeches) — W. E. Thorn
    No. 10928s
PLAY BALL! — James Hefley   No. 9797s
PRAYER — CONVERSING WITH GOD — Rosalind Rinker
    No. 10716s
HOW TO ENJOY THE CHRISTIAN LIFE—Don Mainprize   No. 10106s
THESE MY PEOPLE — Lillian Dickson   No. 9524s
LIFE IS FOR LIVING — Betty Carlson   No. 9384s
SCIENCE RETURNS TO GOD — James H. Jauncey   No. 9927s
NEVER A DULL MOMENT — Eugenia Price   No. 10584s
THE BIBLE FOR TODAY'S WORLD — W. A. Criswell   No. 9426s

160 pages each, 89c

ABOVE OURSELVES — James H. Jauncey   No. 9950s
BECOMING A CHRISTIAN — Rosalind Rinker   No. 10718s
BUT GOD! — V. Raymond Edman   No. 9595s
FIND OUT FOR YOURSELF — Eugenia Price   No. 10603s
LIVING CAN BE EXCITING — Aaron N. Meckel   No. 12280s
THE SAVING LIFE OF CHRIST — W. Ian Thomas   No. 10980s
YOUR CHILD — Anna B. Mow   No. 12256s
SAY 'YES' TO LIFE — Anna B. Mow   No. 10383s
KNOWING GOD'S SECRETS — John Hunter   No. 9883s
THEY FOUND THE SECRET — V. Raymond Edman   No. 9564s
WE'RE NEVER ALONE — Eileen Guder   No. 9710s
MAN TO MAN — Richard C. Halverson   No. 6818s
LIMITING GOD — John Hunter   No. 4702s

192 pages each, 98c

A WOMAN'S WORLD — Clyde Narramore   No. 12230s
HELLBENT FOR ELECTION — P. Speshock   No. 10830s
LIFE AND LOVE — Clyde Narramore   No. 10412s
YOUNG ONLY ONCE — Clyde Narramore   No. 10414s
HOW TO WIN OVER WORRY — John Haggai   No. 9740s
GAMES FOR ALL OCCASIONS — Carlson and Anderson   No. 9051s

Approximately 256 pages each, 98c

WOMAN TO WOMAN — Eugenia Price   No. 10589s
PILGRIM'S PROGRESS — John Bunyan   No. 6610s
LET MY HEART BE BROKEN — Richard Gehman   No. 9694s